THE WORLD ECONOMY

THE WORLD ECONOMY

GLOBAL TRADE POLICY 2007

Edited by
David Greenaway

Blackwell
Publishing

BLACKWELL PUBLISHING
350 Main Street, Malden, MA 02148-5020, USA
9600 Garsington Road, Oxford OX4 2DQ, UK
550 Swanston Street, Carlton, Victoria 3053, Australia

First published 2008 by Blackwell Publishing Ltd

1   2008

ISBN: 978-1-4051-7707-8 (paperback)

A catalogue record for this title is available from the British Library.

Set in 11/13 Times
by Graphicraft Limited, Hong Kong

For further information on
Blackwell Publishing, visit our website:
www.blackwellpublishing.com

Contents

Foreword

Each year *The World Economy* publishes an issue dedicated to developments in global trade policy. That issue always includes a number of ingredients: evaluation of a range of WTO Trade Policy Reviews; a regional feature; and a 'special feature' devoted to a current issue. Because of the interest in this particular issue of the journal, it is always published also as a stand alone book.

Global Trade Policy 2007 includes Trade Policy Reviews of Malaysia, the United States and Trinidad and Tobago. This year's Special Focus is on the Doha Round, with contributions on not only what is at stake, but also possible outcomes. We also include an important agenda setting paper on Trade Preferences, with a focus on how they can help Africa diversify its exports.

I am grateful to the contributors to this volume for preparing an excellent set of papers and to Blackwell for expeditious publication.

1

Malaysia – Trade Policy Review 2006

Bala Ramasamy and Matthew Yeung

1. INTRODUCTION

ESPITE being a small economy, Malaysia is the 20th largest trading nation in the world. In fact, Malaysia's total trade is larger than that of Indonesia, New Zealand, Poland and Turkey. Openness to trade has been the prime contributor to Malaysia's economic performance since the 1960s. It is for this reason that the WTO Trade Policy Review (TPR) is an important document. It provides an impartial view of the Malaysian economy and its trading policies. While larger economies may not consider the TPR to be of much value (Prusa, 2005), for Malaysia, it serves as an effective metric to gauge an outsider perspective of its trade policies as it allows trading partners an opportunity to raise policy issues that affect bilateral trade and investment activities.

In the 2006 TPR, several issues were raised *vis-à-vis* Malaysia's trade and investment policies. These include protection given to local car manufacturers, the high proportion of unbound tariffs, intellectual property rights (IPR), liberalisation of the services sector and government procurement issues. In this paper we address some of these concerns. In Section 2 we provide an update of the Malaysian economy. We emphasise the issue of competitiveness and areas that need immediate attention. The following section considers Malaysia's engagement in regional and bilateral free trade agreements – an area that has seen major changes in trade policy since the last TPR. In the final section we briefly address the issue of Malaysia's tariff protection.

2. THE MALAYSIAN ECONOMY: PERFORMANCE AND PROSPECTS

During the period 2001–05, the Malaysian economy together with other countries in the region had to deal with several exogenous shocks. For an economy

1

that is small and open, the 9/11 terrorist attacks in 2001 and the related wars in Afghanistan and Iraq, the Bali bombings in 2003, the severe acute respiratory syndrome (SARS) in 2003, the Indian Ocean tsunami in 2004 and the crude oil price upsurge in 2004–06 created significant negative impacts. Despite these, the Malaysian economy had an average annual growth rate of 4.5 per cent during this period, marginally higher than the targeted 4.2 per cent in the 8th Malaysia Plan (8MP). In 2005 and the first half of 2006, average economic growth was at 5.35 per cent per quarter (Ministry of Finance, 2006).

The services sector was the major contributor to economic growth with an average annual growth rate of 6.1 per cent, followed by manufacturing at 4.1 per cent, agriculture, forestry, livestock and fisheries at 3.0 per cent and mining at 2.6 per cent. On the demand side, domestic demand continued as in previous years to be a driver of the economy. In 2005, domestic demand was responsible for nearly 92 per cent of the GDP. Government consumption and investment played an important role, making up nearly 30 per cent of GDP. During the 8MP, exports grew at an annual rate of 7.4 per cent compared to import growth of 6.9 per cent. During the first half of 2006, both imports and exports were growing at double-digit rates. In terms of composition of trade, there has been little change since the last TPR report. Manufactured exports still make up the lion's share, accounting for more than 80 per cent in 2005. Among manufactured goods, electrical and electronics (E&E) make up 65.8 per cent, down from a high of 72.5 per cent in 2000. This over-dependence on the E&E sector, as highlighted in the TPR, as well as commodity and mineral exports, increases the vulnerability of the Malaysian economy to foreign demand fluctuations. It is precisely for this reason that Malaysia continues to pursue both a liberal multilateral and regi-lateral trade and investment regime that promotes a stable international environment. In addition, the diversification of Malaysia's external sector to include services exports has been actively promoted. Chief among these are tourism and business process outsourcing.

In 2006, Malaysia launched its 9th Malaysia Plan (9MP), an economic blueprint that would take the nation to 2010. This aims to take the country closer to its aspiration of reaching developed nation status by 2020. The 9MP is organised along five major thrusts (EPU, 2006):

Thrust 1: To move the economy up the value chain. Supporting strategies include achieving higher value added and total factor productivity in manufacturing, services and agricultural sectors; generating new sources of wealth in technology and knowledge-intensive sectors; and expanding the international market for Malaysian goods and services.

Thrust 2: To raise the capacity for knowledge and innovation and nurture 'first class mentality'. Strategies here include improving access to and the quality of the education system and enhancing R&D capabilities.

TABLE 1
Malaysia: IMD's World Competitiveness Indices

Year	2002	2003	2004	2005	2006
Overall Ranking	24	21	16	28	23
Economic Ranking	29	25	16	8	11
Government Efficiency	19	14	16	26	20
Business Efficiency	24	18	13	25	20
Infrastructure	31	31	30	34	31
Total Countries	49	59	60	60	61

Source: IMD World Competitiveness Yearbook 2006.

Thrust 3: To address persistent socio-economic inequalities constructively and productively. The plan aims to halve the incidence of overall poverty to 2.8 per cent and address regional and ethnic income disparities.

Thrust 4: To improve the standard and sustainability of the quality of life. Improvements in housing, health care, transportation systems, energy and water supply are focus areas.

Thrust 5: To strengthen the institutional and implementation capacity. Promotion of good governance both in the private and public sectors and the enhancement of the public service delivery system will be emphasised.

These major goals of the 9MP are timely, particularly Thrusts 1 and 2 when one considers the level of competitiveness of Malaysia *vis-à-vis* other countries. In 2005, there was uproar in political and economic circles when Malaysia slumped to 28th position in the IMD's World Competitiveness Index (see Table 1). In 2006, however, there was a slight improvement. When one considers the various categories of the Competitiveness Index, *Government* and *Business* efficiency seem to be the main culprits since Malaysia was worse in nearly all criteria in sub-categories like *Business Legislation* and *Institutional Framework*. Among the more striking indicators was the number of days to start up a new business which increased from 31 days in 2004 to 57 days in 2005. Indicators that measure corruption, red tape and transparency, all fell in 2005, although the ratings were back to the 2004 levels in the 2006 report.

However, among the four categories, *Infrastructure* is the area where Malaysia is at its weakest (ranked 31 in 2006). In particular, Malaysia is lacking in scientific infrastructure and the health and environment sub-categories. Table 2 shows the R&D expenditures and R&D personnel per capita for Malaysia and other Asian countries. It is clear that the proportion of R&D in Malaysia is at the level of a lower-middle-income country and behind more developed economies like Singapore, Taiwan and Korea. Table 2 also shows a critical cause of Malaysia's

TABLE 2

R&D and Higher Education Achievement, Selected Countries

Countries	Total Expenditure on R&D Per Capita, 2003 or 2004 (USD)	Total R&D Personnel Per Capita, 2003 or 2004, per 1,000 People	Percentage Population with Tertiary Education for Persons Aged 25–34, 2003
China	18.28	0.89	
Hong Kong	161.47	2.48	37.40
India			9.51
Indonesia			5.00
Japan	1,060.33	6.91	52.00
Korea	402.61	4.04	47.00
Malaysia	29.25	0.70	18.00
New Zealand	230.43	5.34	32.00
Philippines			17.00
Singapore	566.72	6.01	49.00
Taiwan	343.99	5.70	43.20
Thailand	6.98	0.67	18.00

Source: IMD World Competitiveness Yearbook 2006.

performance in R&D, namely the education system. Thus, in its quest for developed nation status, the goal of increasing and improving access to tertiary education is critical. No doubt, the Malaysian government realises this. Over the last few years, the number of public universities has been increased such that today nearly every state in the country is home to at least one public university. Tertiary education has also been privatised to the extent that hundreds of private tertiary institutions operate side-by-side with their public counterparts. Thus, improving access to tertiary education has definitely improved. However, it is important that equal attention is given to the quality of education so that the output of the system is not mere numbers but contributes effectively to the development of the country. Failure to emphasise quality may result in similar challenges faced by India and China where the McKinsey Global Institute found only 10 per cent of its graduates are considered employable by multinationals (Farrell et al., 2005).

The declining competitiveness of Malaysia in 2005 should not have come as a surprise since a report by the World Bank in the same year highlighted similar findings. World Bank (2005) was based on the Malaysia Productivity and Investment Climate Survey of 1,151 firms conducted in 2002–03. The objective of the study was to identify the key obstacles to competitiveness from firms' perspectives. The report identified two crucial weaknesses that hinder the level of competitiveness and the investment climate, namely the regulatory burden and skills and innovation capability shortage. Despite having an investment climate that was better than most dynamic regions in China, Malaysian firms still had difficulties when hiring both local and foreign workers due to skill shortages and bureaucratic procedures. In fact, the report states that in the services sector, regulatory restrictions in Malaysia were greater than the average for Asia, Latin America and OECD countries, thus increasing the cost of doing business. As for skill shortages, firms identified insufficient supply of university graduates as a key factor. Acknowledging that the Malaysian government was already addressing these issues, the report calls for:

a. A further strengthening of the investment climate by reducing the high cost of the regulatory burden.
b. An increase in tertiary education enrolment and access to the international labour supply pool.
c. Raising the quality of secondary and tertiary education, in particular English language and IT proficiency.
d. Encouraging greater training activities by firms.
e. Strengthening the National Innovation System by promoting greater firm-institution collaboration and accelerating patent-granting procedures.

International competition will get stiffer as globalisation and trade liberalisation gather momentum (Ariff, 2005). Being competitive is relative. Although Malaysia was once considered among the most competitive countries in Asia, there has to be a realisation that other countries like China, India, Vietnam and even neighbours like Indonesia and Thailand are putting their houses in order. These countries have larger markets and better access to resources.

Take, for instance, SITC72 (Electrical Machinery), Malaysia's single largest manufactured export item. Figure 1 shows the revealed comparative advantage (RCA) for Malaysia and China. In Panel A, we note that Malaysia's RCA has not improved since 1992. On the other hand, China's has been on an upward trend since it became a player in the international economy. Panel B shows the RCA of the two countries in the US market. The declining position of Malaysia is obvious. Since the mid-1980s, Malaysia's comparative advantage has consistently dropped in the US market. In 2002, it lost its market position to China.

Figure 2 shows the results of a correspondence analysis of Malaysia's five largest export markets – the United States, Japan, Singapore, China and the Netherlands (shown in circles). The diamonds are Malaysia's competitors in these markets. Consider the US and Singapore markets. Malaysia's main competitors in these markets are China and Japan as the two countries are the closest to the two markets in the correspondence map. Similarly, Malaysia's main competitors in Japan and China are Korea, Taiwan and Thailand as these three countries are the closest to the two markets in the correspondence map. The result of the correspondence analysis underscores the challenge faced by Malaysia. On the one hand, it has to compete against China – the world's low-cost producer – and on the other it has to challenge Taiwan, Korea and Japan – countries known for their innovation and productivity. Malaysia cannot afford to bask in its former

FIGURE 1
Malaysia and China: Revealed Comparative Advantage for Electrical Machinery (SITC72)

Panel A: RCA World

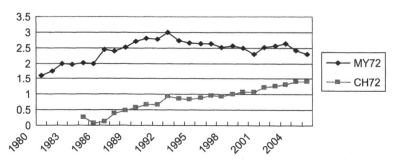

Notes:
MY72 = (Malaysia's exports of SITC72 to the World/Malaysia's exports of all goods to the World)/(World's exports of SITC72/World's exports of all goods).
CH72 = (China's exports of SITC72 to the World/China's exports of all goods to the World)/(World's exports of SITC72/World's exports of all goods).

Panel B: RCA in the US Market

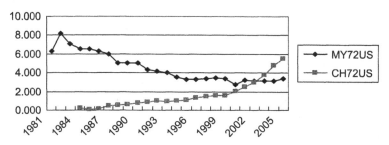

Notes:
MY72US = (Malaysia's exports of SITC72 to the US/Malaysia's exports of all goods to the US)/(US's imports of SITC72 from the World/US's imports of all goods from the World).
CH72US = (China's exports of SITC72 to the US/China's exports of all goods to the US)/(US's imports of SITC72 from the World/US's imports of all goods from the World).

glory. To face these challenges, Malaysia will need to re-focus its efforts into reducing the cost of doing business by increasing productivity and creating a better investment climate. These two strategies would have to be the mantra of economic policies if Malaysia is to regain its position in the world market.

3. REGIONAL AND BILATERAL TRADING ARRANGEMENTS

If there is one area of trade policy that has seen a major change between the last TPR in 2001 and the current one, it has to be the extent to which Malaysia

FIGURE 2
Malaysia's Competitors in International Markets

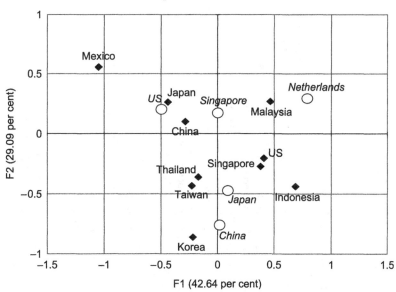

Notes:
Malaysia's top 200 export product categories, the top 200 importers by categories, and the top three competitors in each category were obtained from the trade map developed by the International Trade Centre UNCTAD/WTO. This information showed that the USA, China, Singapore, Japan and the Netherlands ranked among the top five importers of Malaysian goods. From the list of competitors, the top nine competitors were identified. They are the USA, Indonesia, Singapore, China, Taiwan, Japan, Korea, Thailand and the Free Trade Zones. We set up a contingency table with the top five importers as the row and the top nine competitors together with Malaysia as columns. The cells are filled with the frequency counts of the corresponding competitors who ranked top three in the corresponding markets. One simple way to visualise this contingency table is to plot the information onto a bi-plot using correspondence analysis. Correspondence analysis is a method for representing data in an Euclidean space so that the patterns and structures can be visually analysed.

has been involved in bilateral and regional trading arrangements via its membership in the Association of South East Asian Nations (ASEAN). The noodle bowl (Baldwin, 2006) that Malaysia is involved in comprises 18 countries – ASEAN-9, China, Japan, Korea, India, Australia, New Zealand, Pakistan, Chile and the United States. The ASEAN Free Trade Area (AFTA) and the ASEAN China FTA (ACFTA) are perhaps the most advanced among these while other agreements are still at various negotiation stages. See Table 3 for an updated status report. Although these 18 countries account for 71.5 per cent of Malaysia's total trade in 2005, clearly some FTAs are more important than others, namely agreements involving ASEAN, the United States, Japan, China and Korea.

Two events could have precipitated the shift towards FTAs. An obvious one has to be the stalemate of the Doha Round. It must be noted that in the mid-1990s,

TABLE 3
Bilateral and Regional Trading Agreements Involving Malaysia

Partner Country(ies)	Agreements	Status	Proportion of Trade in 2005 (Per cent)
ASEAN	a. ASEAN Framework Agreement on Services b. ASEAN Free Trade Area (AFTA)	a. Negotiations are ongoing. Mutual Recognition Arrangements (MRAs) is the most recent development which enables the qualifications of professional services suppliers to be mutually recognised by member countries, thus facilitating easier flow of professional services providers in the ASEAN region. Areas currently being negotiated and considered for possible conclusion of MRAs include Engineering, Architecture, Accountancy, Surveying and Tourism. b. Reduction of tariff was completed with exceptions by the ASEAN-6 including Malaysia in 2003.	25.24
China	ASEAN–China Free Trade Area (ACFTA)	Signed in 2002 and began to take full effect from 1 July 2005 with a complete establishment of the FTA in 2010 for older ASEAN members including Malaysia. Negotiations for FTA in services and investment are ongoing.	8.79
India	a. Malaysia India Comprehensive Economic Partnership Agreement b. ASEAN–India Framework Agreement on Comprehensive Economic Cooperation	a. Feasibility study for a comprehensive Economic Cooperation Agreement is now complete. b. Framework agreement signed in 2003, with a target realisation date of 2011 for the older ASEAN members. Though an agreement for FTA in goods was expected for January 2006, it has been delayed to January 2007 due to difficulties in defining the rules of origin clause.	1.98
Pakistan	Malaysia–Pakistan Free Trade Agreement	Negotiations ongoing.	0.003

Partner	Agreement	Status	Value
Australia	a. ASEAN–ANZCERTA Free Trade Agreement b. Australia–Malaysia Free Trade Agreement	a. Negotiations started in early 2005 with a view of completion in 2007. Agreement in non-tariff barriers, services and investment also being negotiated. b. Negotiations supposed to conclude in mid-2006 but difficulties remain in the areas of Government Procurement, Competition Policy and Intellectual Property.	2.71
New Zealand	a. Malaysia–New Zealand Free Trade Agreement b. ASEAN–ANZCERTA Free Trade Agreement	a. Negotiations have been suspended due to difficulties in the areas of services, Government Procurement, Labour and Environment. b. as a above	0.34
Korea	a. Malaysia–Korea Free Trade Agreement b. ASEAN–Korea Free Trade Agreement	a. FTA in goods completed in 2005. The Agreement in Services and Investment still being negotiated. b. FTA for trade in goods ongoing. First tranche of tariff reduction/elimination started in July 2006. Negotiations on Trade in Services to be concluded by 31 December, 2006.	4.09
United States	a. Malaysia–nited States Trade and Investment Framework b. Malaysia–United States Free Trade Area	a. Agreement signed in 2004. Cooperation ongoing. b. Negotiations launched in March 2006 and expected to be completed in early 2007.	16.63
Japan	a. Japan–Malaysia Economic Partnership Agreement b. ASEAN–Japan Comprehensive Economic Partnership	a. Formal negotiation started in 2003 and Agreement signed in 2005. Cooperation ongoing. b. Agreement involves both an FTA in goods and services. Negotiations are ongoing with a targeted FTA in 2012.	11.67
Chile	Malaysia–Chile Free Trade Agreement	Negotiations ongoing.	0.09

Source: http://www.aseansec.org

Malaysia as well as other countries in East Asia pursued a unilateral and non-preferential route to trade liberalisation (Pangestu and Gooptu, 2004). This was to facilitate the offshoring strategies of Japanese firms initially, followed by Hong Kong, Korean, Taiwanese and Singaporean firms at a later stage (known as the flying geese model; Baldwin, 2006). By pursuing a multilateral trade liberalisation strategy, Malaysia became a choice location for offshoring activities among multinationals. Second, the proposal for an East Asian economic bloc in 1990 by Malaysia's Prime Minister Mahathir was opposed by the United States and its allies, but the idea of an ASEAN-China Free Trade Area proposed by China's Zhu Rongji in 2000 had a catalytic effect in trade policies among all countries in the region. Singapore, in particular, started to actively pursue FTAs with a wide range of countries including the United States, Australia and Japan (Thangavelu and Toh, 2006). To be left out of the growing web of preferential deals was not an option that Malaysia was willing to risk.

A cursory glance at Table 3 reveals two important findings. First, agreements involving goods seem much easier to conclude than those which are more comprehensive, particularly involving services and investment. For instance, the ACFTA in goods took about three years for a blueprint to be agreed on, whereas the agreement involving the services and investment component of the ACFTA seems to be ongoing. Second, agreements with other developing countries are concluded in a faster time frame compared to those involving developed economies. As with trade agreements worldwide (Roy et al., 2006), Malaysia's trade deals involving developed countries are more comprehensive, i.e. involving services and investments, and thus are more complicated. If agreement between two countries on these issues face difficulties, one could only imagine how a comprehensive multilateral agreement can be reached at the WTO level. Thus, separating the agreements into goods, services and investment seems to be a faster way forward.

The costs and benefits of RTAs over WTO-type multilateral agreements have been discussed extensively elsewhere (see, for example, OECD, 2002). For Malaysia, the official reason for the pursuit of FTAs, both bilateral and regional, as stated in the TPR includes: '1) ... *to maximize all opportunities for enhancing the country's economic growth* ... [p. 24]; 2) ... *to provide mutual benefits among signatories, are consistent with WTO rules, and allow sufficient flexibility to address specific sectoral and development concerns* ... [p. 24]; and 3) ... *to strengthen the export market base* ... [p. 134]'.

To what extent have these objectives been fulfilled? It is perhaps a little too early for an analysis to be undertaken. However, if all FTAs are to be as successful as the AFTA – the oldest amongst the FTAs – there are valid reasons to be sceptical. Baldwin (2006) claims that utilisation rates under AFTA are extremely low. Analysis by JETRO (2003) shows that only 4.1 per cent of Malaysia's exports within AFTA enjoyed preferential tariffs (the Common Effective Preferential Tariff – CEPT). Similarly, only 11.2 per cent of Thailand's imports from

AFTA were under the CEPT. A margin of preference that is too low compared to the administrative cost involved in applying for the CEPT is blamed for the lack of motivation among traders to utilise the CEPT. One could argue then that FTAs involving goods for Malaysia do not produce any tangible results since the average tariff rate on goods is already low at 8.1 per cent (TPR, p. 36). This implies that Malaysia's FTAs could only achieve the stated objectives by pursuing free trade in sectors where reduction in trade barriers make a substantial difference for businesses, in particular the services sector.

Malaysia, as well as her ASEAN neighbours, tend to follow the positive listing (or bottom-up) approach (Roy et al., 2006), where members in an agreement list the national treatment, market access commitments and conditions under which a foreign supplier of services can enter a particular market. Upon further negotiation, these conditions are eased. The intention is that over a period of time, liberalisation is progressively achieved. However, commitments made are binding. Although this approach promotes transparency, i.e. the rules of market entry are clearly laid out, negotiations to further liberalise trade and investment policies can be time consuming. The negative listing approach as pursued by the US is considered a faster approach. If Malaysia and its partners continue the former approach, the extent of further liberalisation will be directly proportional to the political will of member countries.

An issue highlighted by many trading partners in the TPR is the extent of liberalisation in the services sector. The principal barriers to market access in the services sector are listed in Table IV.11 in the TPR. A more detailed list is available from the WTO Services Database Output. Ownership restrictions dominate the type of barriers. Market entry into most services sectors are either restricted to 'natural persons' or 'through a locally incorporated joint-venture corporation with Malaysian individuals or Malaysian-controlled corporations'. Although Malaysia acknowledges the positive effect on productivity as a result of increasing foreign ownership, there are political and social implications of liberalising the market. Thus, limiting foreign ownership is seen as a strategy to balance productivity and social imbalances. In this regard, Malaysia remains a developing country that prefers to improve its competitive advantage before being subjected to international competition.

It is not likely that this strategy will be drastically reversed. As a result, the speed at which FTA agreements in services and investment can be concluded depend on the extent to which domestic firms are capable of being competitive in the international market. As competitive advantage is established, conditions for entry and ownership restrictions are gradually eased. For instance, Malaysia issued three new Islamic banking licences to foreign banks because it was confident that the two domestic Islamic banks were ready for competition.

It follows then that the most effective way to encourage developing countries like Malaysia to liberalise the services sector is to promote efforts that would improve the competitive advantage of domestic firms. Thus, agreements that build capabilities in domestic industries are encouraged. The Japan-Malaysia Economic Partnership Agreement (JMEPA) which promotes cooperation and collaboration in manufacturing related services, ICT and biotechnology and facilitates the inclusion of Malaysian SMEs into the manufacturing supply chains of Japanese MNCs, serves as a good blueprint for future agreements. In addition, the fact that many FTAs in services are much deeper and wider in scope (Roy et al., 2006) than the GATS provides further impetus for more of such FTAs.

An alternative method of liberalising the services sector is to use corporate profit tax rates as a form of tariff. By imposing a higher profit tax on wholly owned foreign services enterprises, only the most efficient entities would be interested in setting up offices in Malaysia. That would ensure that only the best practices are used and there are opportunities for these to spill over to domestic entities. This could help in the development of local talent, and create domestic enterprises that are also competitive. Sceptics may argue that the goal of offering national treatment to all types of enterprises, whether local or foreign, may be compromised. However, one has to remember that in the past, for trade in goods, import quotas were 'tariffied' before tariff reduction took place. In like manner, by imposing different profit rates, this could be the first step towards liberalising the services sector. This approach could be implemented at an FTA level like AFTA before being opened up to third countries. We accept that this approach may require further deliberation.

4. TARIFF PROTECTION

One main issue raised by several commentators in the TPR was the tariff protection practised by Malaysia. The comments revolved around the high protection given to the local car producers (Japan, Taiwan and the US); the high proportion of tariffs which were still unbound (Japan, Hong Kong, EU, US, Korea, Canada and Brazil), and the applied[1] tariff levels which were still high on some goods (EU, US, Korea and Pakistan).

In this section we deal with Malaysia's tariff protection issue. We limit this to tariff-related protection and ignore other trade barriers like import quotas, standards and other non-tariff barriers (NTBs). We considered three items in tariff protection: applied tariffs, the proportion of unbound tariff lines to total tariff lines, and the level of bound tariffs. These items were selected because a common issue raised by the commentators in the TPR relates to the gap between applied

---

[1] All discussion refers to nominal rather than effective tariffs. For an evaluation of the role of each in policy appraisal, see Greenaway and Milner (2003).

tariffs and bound tariffs on the one hand, as well as the high and unchanged proportion of unbound tariffs on the other. In 2005, for example, Malaysia still had not bound more than one-third of its tariff lines.

We created an index of tariff protection by taking into account the three items as follows:

a. The proportion of bound products to total number of products in the category. High proportions indicate a higher degree of openness or a lower degree of protection.

b. The inverse of applied tariffs. A higher level of applied tariff indicates a higher degree of protection while its reverse would indicate a greater degree of openness.

c. The level of inverse bound tariffs. Higher levels of bound tariff indicate a greater degree of protection and vice versa.

All three values were standardised to between 0 and 1. We summed these components to create our index of tariff protection. In other words, all three items were given equal weights. The full mean scores for all product categories under HS2, weighted by the number of lines under the corresponding HS6 category, is given in the Appendix. We display the 15 most protected product categories in Figure 3. A low score indicates a higher degree of protection.

FIGURE 3
Malaysia: Tariff Protection Index

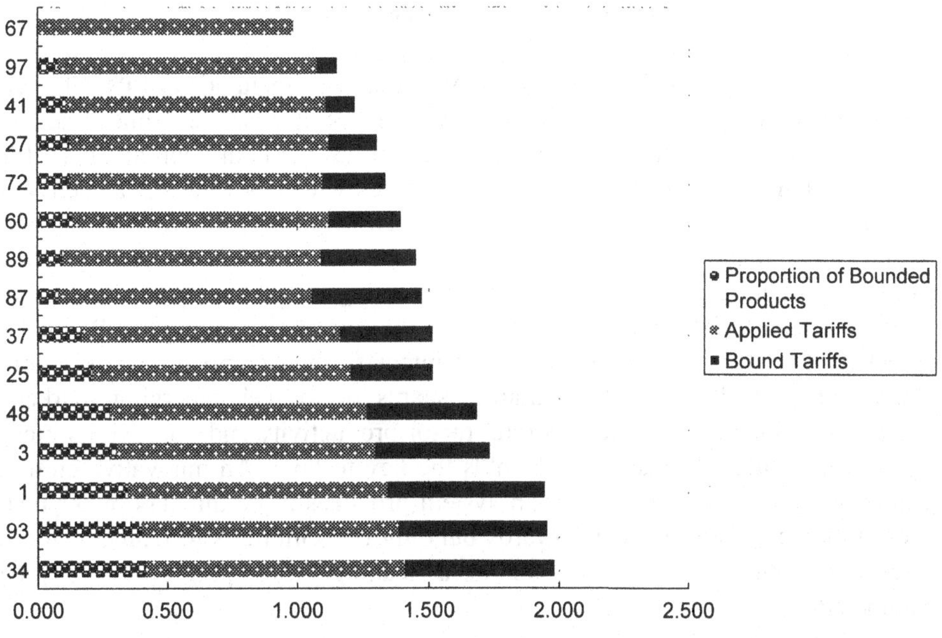

Figure 3 shows that the degree of protection due to applied tariffs is not substantially different from one product category to another. The differences lie in the other two items of the index. For instance, HS2 category 67 (Prepared feathers and downs, artificial flowers and articles of human hair) is the product category with the highest degree of protection. Though the level of applied tariff may be similar to other categories, all its product lines are unbound. Similarly, the other product categories in Figure 3 are protected by their high degree of 'unboundness', and even if they are bound the levels are high. Thus, the explanation given by the Malaysian trade representative that the reason for the large gap between applied tariffs and bound tariffs was due to a decrease in the former (TPR, p. 161) ignores the fact that the degree of protection changes little. The fact that tariffs could be increased to the bound level is the issue of concern.

Pursuing developmental goals as the reason for not binding a large number of tariff lines is also clarified in Figure 3. Among the 15 product categories, nine of these (HS2 categories 1, 3, 25, 34, 48, 60, 67, 72 and 87) are most likely protected to safeguard domestic industries. HS2 categories 27, 37, 89 and 97 are probably protected for tax revenue purposes while category 93 is due to civil protection. Whether protecting domestic industries will result in the development of the sectors stated earlier remains to be seen. Surely, the protection of these industries through tariffs has to be complemented with other policies that would raise the level of competitiveness?

5. CONCLUSION

The next five years will be critical for Malaysia. The maturation of the Chinese economy, the emergence of the Indian and the Vietnamese economies and the strengthening of the Thai and Indonesian economies are both boon and bane for Malaysia. On the one hand, export market shares will be further threatened. On the other, growth in these economies increases opportunities for Malaysian businesses. Pursuing FTAs or multilateral trade liberalisation policies with the hope of widening the export base, or protecting certain sectors by erecting tariff and non-tariff barriers aimed at developing those sectors, will not be effective if Malaysian businesses do not intensify their competitiveness within the region. Whether to protect market shares or to seek emerging markets, Malaysia will need to increase its total factor productivity and improve its innovative capabilities. Human capital holds the key to both. An innovative culture can only be created if the education system produces more thinkers rather than mere followers. The first step towards building this culture is to realise that the days when Malaysia can be considered a 'leading' developing nation may be numbered.

APPENDIX 1

Tariff Protection

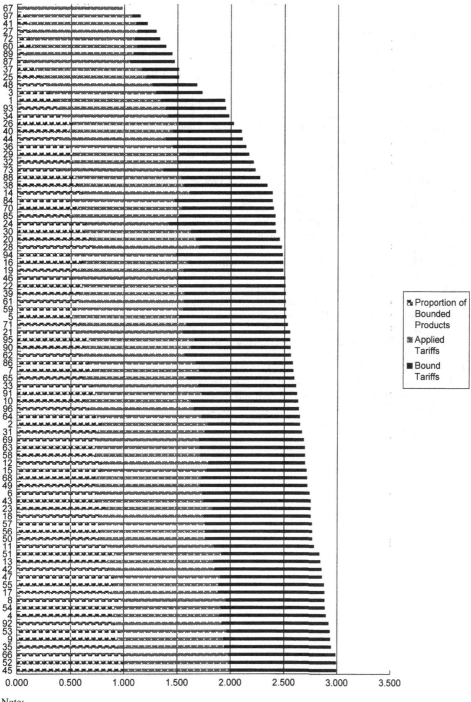

Note:

Y-axis = Sectors (HS2); X-axis = Tariff Protection Index.

REFERENCES

Ariff, M. (2005), 'The Drivers of Competitiveness in Malaysia', *The Australian APEC Studies Centre Conference on an Australia/Malaysia Free Trade Agreement* (The Marriott Hotel, Melbourne, 10 March).

Baldwin, R. E. (2006), 'Multilateralising Regionalism: Spaghetti Bowls as Building Blocs on the Path to Global Free Trade', *The World Economy*, **29**, 11, 1451–518.

BNM (2006), 'Economic and Financial Developments in Malaysia in the Third Quarter of 2006' (Press Release, Bank Negara Malaysia, 23 November, http://www.bnm.gov.my).

EPU (2006), *Ninth Malaysia Plan* (Economic Planning Unit, Prime Minister's Department, http: http://www.epu.jpm.my/rm9/html/english.htm).

Farrell, D., M. Laboissière, J. Rosenfeld, S. Stürze and F. Umezawa (2005), *The Emerging Global Labor Market: Part II – The Supply of Offshore Talent in Services* (McKinsey Global Institute).

Greenaway, D. and C. R. Milner (2003), 'Effective Protection, Policy Appraisal and Trade Policy Reform', *The World Economy*, **26**, 4, 441–56.

JETRO (2003), 'Current Status of AFTA and Corporate Responses' (November, JETRO, Japan).

Ministry of Finance (2006), *Quarterly Update Malaysian Economy* (http://www.treasury.gov.my).

OECD (2002), *The Relationship between Regional Trade Agreements and the Multilateral Trading System* (Paris: OECD).

Pangestu, M. and S. Gooptu (2004), 'New Regionalism: Options for East Asia', in K. Krumm and H. Kharas (eds.), *East Asia Integrates: A Trade Policy Agenda for Shared Growth* (Washington, DC: World Bank and Oxford University Press), 39–57.

Prusa, T. J. (2005), '2004 Trade Policy Review – The United States', *The World Economy: Global Trade Policy 2005*, **28**, 9, 1263–76.

Roy, M., J. Marchetti and H. Lim (2006), 'Services Liberalisation in the New Generation of Preferential Trade Agreements (PTAs): How Much Further than the GATS?', WTO Staff Working Paper (http://www.wto.org).

Thangavelu, S. M. and M.-H. Toh (2006), 'Bilateral "WTO Plus" Free Trade Agreements: The WTO Trade Policy Review of Singapore 2004', in D. Greenaway (ed.), *The World Economy: Global Trade Policy 2005* (Oxford: Blackwell Publishing).

World Bank (2005), *Malaysia: Firm Competitiveness, Investment Climate and Growth* (Poverty Reduction, Economic Management and Financial Sector Unit, East Asia and Pacific Region, The World Bank).

2

Allies and Friends: The Trade Policy Review of the United States, 2006

Rodney D. Ludema

1. INTRODUCTION

IT'S a good thing the United States government believes that democracy, rule of law and economic development abroad are keys to its national security. For notwithstanding the occasional catastrophe accompanying US military actions in the name of democracy, this belief has fostered policies on the economic front that have contributed to the prosperity of billions of people throughout the world. The multilateral trading system is a product of this synergy of economic and security concerns. During the creation and critical early years of the GATT, the US helped sustain the system in large measure because of a heightened concern about its national security during the Cold War. With the collapse of Communism and subsequent absorption of many former adversaries into the WTO, the US looked poised for a return to civilian life, its trade policy focused on mundane commercial interests like everyone else. However, the events of 11 September, 2001, cut this respite short. With national security now back at the top of the US foreign policy agenda, it is an open question whether the WTO system will be better or worse off as a result. This question forms the subtext of the 2006 WTO *Trade Policy Review* (TPR) *of the United States.*

The 2006 TPR is the eighth review of the US since the TPR programme began on a provisional basis in 1989. *Trade Policy Reviews* are periodic status reports by the WTO on the trade-related economic circumstances and policies of its members. They are like audits of each member, evaluating its progress in implementing WTO rules, disciplines and commitments, highlighting compliance problems, and surveying the broader economic situation to presage trouble or opportunities ahead. The purpose is to increase transparency and understanding of each member's trade policies for the benefit of other members, which will hopefully facilitate compliance.

The United States, the European Union, Japan and Canada are reviewed every two years. Other countries are reviewed at either four- or six-year intervals depending on their relative size in world trade. The practice of reviewing larger countries more often makes sense, if we consider that their policies are of greatest importance to other members and that they account for the bulk of the dispute settlement activity. It also makes sense that developing country governments would need more help in understanding the trade policy of developed countries than vice versa. The differential frequency of the reviews has its downside though. Very few alternative sources of information exist about many developing countries, whereas there is plenty of information already available about the US, much of it better than what can be found in the *Reviews*. Indeed, most of what is contained in the TPR of the US is drawn from these other sources. Still, the TPR of the US is useful in drawing it all together and airing the comments of various members.

Each TPR contains three main sections. The first and largest part is a report by the WTO Secretariat. It contains an overview, beginning with the macroeconomic situation, trends in trade and investment, and developments in trade and investment policy, followed by a detailed description of trade policies by measure and sector. The report is intended to be thorough, factual and impartial. The second part is a report by the member being reviewed, in this case the United States. It is not intended to be thorough or impartial (though one hopes it is factually accurate). Instead it focuses on the country's goals, plans and accomplishments and on justifying its more controversial policies. The final section is a summary of the TPR meeting, which contains comments on the Secretariat's report by the United States, comments on the US by an assigned discussant (Amabssador Amina Chawahir Mohamed of Kenya, former Chair of the General Council), and comments by some 30 other members. The most vocal criticisms of US trade policy come from these member comments. However, because each has its own list of grievances, the overall critique lacks coherence and impact. One almost wishes that the discussant and member comments could be combined and distilled into a well-articulated 'dissenting opinion'.

If I were writing the dissent, I would argue that heightened US national security concerns have had both direct and indirect effects that are deleterious to the multilateral trading system. Security concerns have led to an embrace of bilateralism that bears little relation to US commercial interests and will arguably detract from ongoing efforts at multilateral trade liberalisation. Security concerns have also led to a substantial change in customs and inspection procedures for goods bound for the US, which could swamp tariffs in terms of their trade-inhibiting effect. Finally, the unpopularity at home of US military actions abroad has weakened the US President and opened the door for rising protectionism in Congress.

In what follows, I shall touch on only a few of the many issues raised in the TPR, leaving the interested reader to forage it for details on her own. I shall concentrate on areas where I see the most alarming trends and which best illustrate the thesis of my dissent.

2. SOURCES OF RISING PROTECTION

a. *The Twin Deficits and Other Economic Factors*

The Secretariat report begins with a thumbnail sketch of the macroeconomic situation facing the US, based on data up to the third quarter of 2005. On the whole the news is positive, as the US was in the midst of a recovery. The main concern is about fiscal and current account deficits. The federal government deficit reached $412 billion in 2004 and was projected at $333 billion for 2005 (it turned out to be $319 billion), or 3.6 and 2.6 per cent of GDP, respectively. Careful to cite IMF and Congressional Budget Office sources, the report attributes part of the deficit to tax cuts and increased spending on defence and social security. The current account deficit continued to expand through 2004, reaching a record $668 billion, or 5.7 per cent of GDP, and was projected to go higher, despite a depreciating dollar. Both the Federal Reserve and IMF are reported to have declared the inflow of capital supporting this deficit 'unsustainable'. The US's report defended its fiscal policy as an 'appropriate counter-cyclical' measure, and blamed excessive foreign saving for the current account deficit. Several countries, most notably Switzerland, expressed concern that a hard landing would be disruptive to the world economy.

Lacking from the Secretariat's report is any mention of how these economic trends have contributed to increased US protectionism. To my mind, this omission largely defeats the purpose of the economic survey. The current account deficit has unquestionably fuelled protectionism in the US Congress, especially against China. A Bill introduced into the Senate in 2005 by Charles Schumer of New York, on behalf of a bipartisan coalition of senators from manufacturing states (including Presidential hopeful Hillary Clinton), accused China of currency manipulation and called for negotiations aimed at revaluation of the yuan, which if not successful would be answered by a 27.5 per cent across-the-board tariff on Chinese imports. Of course, this Bill did not pass, but other protectionist measures against China, e.g. special safeguards on textiles and clothing, are on the rise.

Also missing is any mention of rising income inequality or loss of manufacturing jobs. While not specific to the 2004–2005 period, wages of unskilled workers have been in decline, both in real terms and in relation to skilled wages, for the past 25 years. This trend is widely acknowledged, even by the Bush administration, which is surprising considering that it is accused of contributing to the problem through tax cuts favouring the rich and other pro-business policies. The elimination of the steel safeguards in early 2004, following a WTO panel ruling, also contributed to Bush's reputation as an enemy of labour and has led to growing scepticism toward trade agreements in Congress.

At the time the TPR was written, participants could not have known that these developments, combined with voter dissatisfaction over the war in Iraq, would help the Democrats take control of Congress and put new constraints on the President's trade agenda. However, protectionist pressures from both parties were clearly present at the time, and the President had already compromised on many key issues to secure trade promotion authority (TPA), such as the inclusion of labour and environmental standards in bilateral trade deals and the expansion of Trade Adjustment Assistance. While these concessions are discussed in the TPR as part of the general trade policy landscape, a frank discussion of their underlying economic and political causes is sorely lacking.

b. Agricultural Subsidies and Administered Protection

Previous TPRs focused heavily on US agricultural subsidies and administered protection. These measures continue to be controversial in the present TPR, but the controversies are muted somewhat by the fact both subsidies and anti-dumping filings were down in 2004, thanks to high prices for crops and steel. However, the US lost several important WTO disputes in these areas. And while it appeared to be complying with most of the rulings, it had not yet repealed the Byrd Amendment at the time of the TPR (it has since).

Although the Secretariat report showed subsidies were down from 2002 to 2004, total government outlays to farmers were projected to shoot up again in 2005 to over US$21 billion, rivalling their 2000 peak (the projection was roughly correct). The increase was driven mostly by a four-fold increase in counter-cyclical payments and a seven-fold increase in ad hoc emergency pay-ments. The 2002 Farm Bill brought the counter-cyclical payments programme back into the US agricultural policy arsenal, after it had been eliminated in 1996. It is decidedly contrary to the goal of reducing trade distortions associated with agricultural support, but with the Doha Round now fading, it is questionable if a WTO agreement will be reached to eliminate them. Meanwhile, Brazil mounted a successful dispute-settlement challenge of the US subsidy programme for upland cotton.

Anti-dumping filings in the US continued to drop throughout the period. There were 39 filings in 2004 and only 12 in 2005, compared with 116 in 2001. As the steel industry accounts for the majority of filings in a typical year, this trend was probably driven by strong demand for steel worldwide. The US steel industry is profitable again, despite the repeal of the 2002 safeguards. Nevertheless, as of June 2005, 274 anti-dumping duties were still in force. On the more systemic level, WTO disputes continue to pummel US administered protection laws. The Anti-dumping Act of 1916, which allowed for civil and criminal penalties against dumpers, and the Byrd Amendment, which distributed revenue from anti-dumping and countervailing duties to successful petitioners, were both found in violation of the WTO anti-dumping agreement. Although it took a long time and numerous retaliatory threats, both laws were eventually repealed. The practice of 'zeroing', which amounts to throwing out all negative dumping margins when computing an average dumping margin, was also challenged in a series of disputes involving Canada, Japan and the EU.

Many in Congress and the administration regard the WTO rulings on US anti-dumping laws, along with earlier rulings to safeguard actions and tax provisions for Foreign Sales Corporations, as rank judicial activism. The Secretariat report cites the House Ways and Means Committee, which oversees the US-administered protection apparatus, as complaining of 'the "gap filling" by panels that read more exacting, and sometimes impractical, requirements into the WTO agreements, particularly with respect to trade remedy laws'. This sentiment has produced a number of effects. First, as a condition for granting TPA, Congress demanded that a principal negotiating objective be to preserve the ability of the United States to vigorously enforce its trade remedy laws.[1] Second, the US built special safeguards for 'sensitive' products, with relaxed requirements on material injury, into its accession agreement with China and its bilateral FTAs. Third, it has created FTA-specific dispute settlement bodies, which give members the option of resolving disputes outside the jurisdiction of WTO panels.[2]

c. New Customs Procedures and Technical Barriers

There are many non-tariff trade barriers mentioned in the TPR. What is new is the proliferation of regulations designed to incorporate security considerations into its import procedures. There are three main programmes. First, under the Trade Act of 2002, all importers are required to transmit information to the Customs and Border Protection agency (CBP) pertaining to US-bound cargo from all modes of transportation prior to departure. CBP uses this information to identify and stop high-risk cargo before it leaves a foreign port. According to the CBP, the costs of meeting the requirements of the Trade Act regulations will be 'substantial' for air carriers (US and foreign) flying cargo into the United States but less so for sea and rail carriers as they make use of electronic filing already. Second, the Container Security Initiative (CSI) of 2002 requires screening and inspection of all US-bound, high-risk containers at the port of departure and the use of tamper-evident seals. The US authorises a limited number of foreign ports

---

[1] The Senate passed a version of TPA containing the so-called Dayton-Craig amendment, which would have excluded from fast-track procedures any provision that would change any US trade remedy law. This provision was ultimately stripped from the final legislation in favour of the language about priorities.
[2] See Busch (2007) for a discussion of these overlapping jurisdictional issues.

to conduct inspections, and the costs to the foreign ports are high.[3] Third, the Bioterrorism Act requires importers to notify the Food and Drug Administration of all US-bound food consignments, and all food manufacturing and handling facilities have to be registered to export to the United States.

These are sweeping changes, and while they may well be necessary, their impact on trade is as yet unknown. Anyone who has been through US airport security lately will appreciate how costly these kinds of regulations can be. The Secretariat's report suggests that, 'an assessment of the economic impact of the new regulations would be valuable to ascertain their actual costs and benefits'. Numerous countries in the TPR meeting echoed that call.

3. THE 'FTA RUSH'

Without question the most notable aspect of US trade policy in recent years has been its embrace of bilateral and regional free trade agreements, or what Japan referred to as an 'FTA Rush'. Besides NAFTA (involving Canada and Mexico, which went into force in 1994) and its FTA with Israel (1985), the US has implemented FTAs with Jordan (2001), Chile (2004), Singapore (2004), Australia (2005), Morocco (2006) and Bahrain (2006). By the time of the TPR meeting, agreements had been signed with Colombia, Peru, Oman and the six countries forming CAFTA-DR (Costa Rica, El Salvador, Guatemala, Honduras, Nicaragua and the Dominican Republic); negotiations were ongoing with Ecuador, Panama, Korea, Malaysia, Thailand, United Arab Emirates and the Southern African Customs Union (South Africa, Botswana, Lesotho, Namibia and Swaziland). Thus, from 2001 to 2006, the number of US FTA partners or imminent partners went from three to 29.

Concerns about the effect of this trend on the multilateral trading system are expressed throughout the TPR. The arguments are familiar. First, there is the argument that bilateralism is a 'stumbling block' to further multilateral liberalisation. In the TPR, this argument can be found in two different versions. One is that bilateral agreements might divert the administrative resources of their members away from multilateral negotiations. The other, made by the EU (speaking from experience one presumes), is that bilateral agreements might compromise domestic political support for further multilateral liberalisation. Second, there is the argument that bilateral agreements harm third countries through trade diversion.

---

[3] Although CBP pays for the expenses of CBP officers stationed in foreign ports, host country officers have to inspect the containers using non-intrusive inspection equipment, physical inspection, or both. Seaports must have gamma- or X-ray imaging equipment, and radiation detection equipment. In addition, ports must establish an automated risk management system, share data with CBP, resolve the security vulnerabilities of their infrastructure, and maintain personnel integrity programmes.

The discussant lamented that discrimination against developing countries is contrary to the goals of the Doha Development Agenda. Finally, there is the 'Spaghetti Bowl' problem, also raised by the discussant, which is the idea that the complexity of preferential tariff rates and rules of origin poses a barrier to trade in its own right.

The US report addresses only the first of these concerns, arguing that rather than being a stumbling block, bilateral and regional agreements serve as 'an incubator and catalyst for multilateral liberalization'. As evidence for this, it cites the many bilateral agreements the US signed in the 1930s and 1940s, which foreshadowed the clauses that ultimately were included in GATT. It goes on to name various provisions contained in its current rash of FTAs, such as tariff-free and quota-free market access, labour and environmental standards, stronger IPR protection, special safeguards and trade facilitation measures, that go beyond current WTO provisions and which 'appear to be adding momentum to global trade liberalization, fostering trade and growth, and stimulating our FTA partners to greater participation in the WTO' (p. 148). Finally, the US flatly rejects the administrative version of the stumbling-block argument, saying that it has found no such tendency among its FTA partners. In fact, it claims to have selected its FTA partners for their 'clear, consistent commitment to WTO-based trade liberalization' (p. 187).

These claims are worth more careful examination. It is certainly true that many of the provisions of the Reciprocal Trade Agreements Act of 1934 (RTAA), under which the US negotiated its pre-GATT bilateral agreements, did profoundly influence the GATT. However, it is difficult to see how this point supports the US case in the current debate. First, at the time of the old US bilaterals, there was no multilateral system to detract from. Second, the bilateral agreements themselves contained the MFN clause, precisely because the US recognised the costs and dangers associated with discrimination. Third, the GATT was created to replace the bilateral agreements, because they were regarded as inadequate and too shaky a foundation for the global trading system. Finally, not all of the provisions that made the jump from the RTAA to the GATT were necessarily helpful to the cause of multilateral liberalisation. Anti-dumping and safeguards provisions come to mind. Likewise, it can be argued that the labour and environmental standards, special safeguards (and perhaps even the stronger IPR protections) contained in current FTAs are not directions the WTO should go (see, e.g., Bhawati, 2005).

Does the US really select its FTA partners on the basis of their commitment to WTO-based trade liberalisation? Answering this question is difficult, because it is hard to measure commitment. However, we might expect commitment to be reflected in a country's record of multilateral trade liberalisation prior to entering FTA negotiations. Though not ideal, a commonly used measure of protection is a country's simple average of applied MFN tariffs over all tariff lines. Figure 1

FIGURE 1
Distributions of Average Applied MFN Tariffs by Country, 2001
(US FTA partners vs non-FTA WTO members)

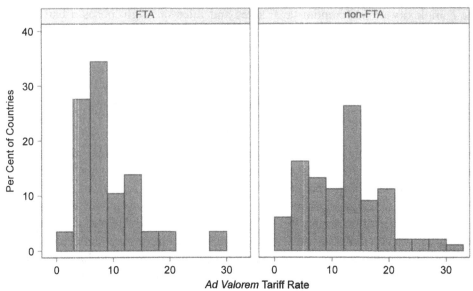

Source: Trends in Applied Average Tariffs: World Bank.

compares the distribution of this measure across US FTA partners to that of other
WTO members for 2001.[4] We see that the preponderance of FTA partners had
average tariffs between five and 15 per cent. The mean is actually 8.9 per cent.
Outliers are Singapore with zero tariffs and Morocco, with an average tariff of
29.2 per cent. For non-FTA countries the picture is similar but with a higher
variance and a mean of 11.7 per cent. About half of the difference in means
between the two groups is due to the presence of least developed countries
(LDCs) in the non-FTA category, which tend to have very high tariffs and also
have free access to the US market through other programmes. Lesotho is the only
US FTA partner classified as an LDC. Taking out LDCs, one cannot reject the
hypothesis that these two samples were drawn from the same distribution.[5] Thus,
despite the lower tariffs of US FTA partners relative to other WTO countries
overall, it seems quite unlikely that the US was selecting partners on this basis.
If it were, it must have applied a very coarse filter, for it chose a number of
countries with tariffs well in excess of the WTO average.

---

[4] Data are from 'Trends in Average Applied Tariff Rates in Developing and Industrial Countries,
1981–2005' by Francis Ng at the World Bank (http://siteresources.worldbank.org/INTRES/
Resources/tar2005.xls). Tariff levels were available for all 29 FTA partners and 101 non-FTA
WTO countries.
[5] This conclusion is based on two non-parametric tests for equality of distributions, namely the
Kolmogorov-Smirnov and Mann-Whitney two-sample tests, with a 10 per cent significance threshold.

FIGURE 2
Distributions of MFN Tariff Cuts by Country, 1994–2001
(US FTA partners vs non-FTA WTO members)

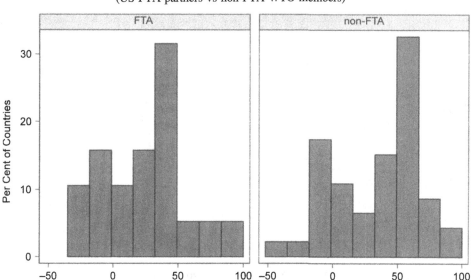

Source: Trends in Applied Average Tariffs: World Bank.

Considering that countries may have reasons for maintaining high initial levels of protection that are unrelated to the WTO process, perhaps a better way to measure commitment to multilateralism would be to look at the percentage tariff reductions countries made following the Uruguay Round. Figure 2 compares the distributions of average applied MFN tariff reductions between 1994 and 2001 for US FTA partners against other WTO members.[6] We see a surprisingly large variance in both groups: some countries actually raised their tariffs by as much as 50 per cent during this period, while others, such as Singapore and Hong Kong, eliminated tariffs entirely. Overall, the FTA group cut tariffs by an average of 26 per cent, while the non-FTA group cut tariffs by 34 per cent. Again this difference in group means is cut in half when LDCs are excluded. Moreover, with or without LDCs, one cannot reject that these two samples come from the same distribution. The same conclusion emerges from Figure 3, which compares more recent cross-country distributions in tariff reductions, 2001–2003. In other words,

---

[6] Post-Uruguay changes were available for 19 FTA partners and 46 non-FTA countries. To increase coverage, changes were computed on the basis of an average of 1993 and 1994 tariffs. Tariff changes between 2001 and 2003 were available for 22 FTA partners and 83 non-FTA countries. The year 2003 was used because it is the last year for which at least 75 per cent of the countries are represented.

FIGURE 3

Distributions of MFN Tariff Cuts by Country, 2001–2003

(US FTA partners vs non-FTA WTO members)

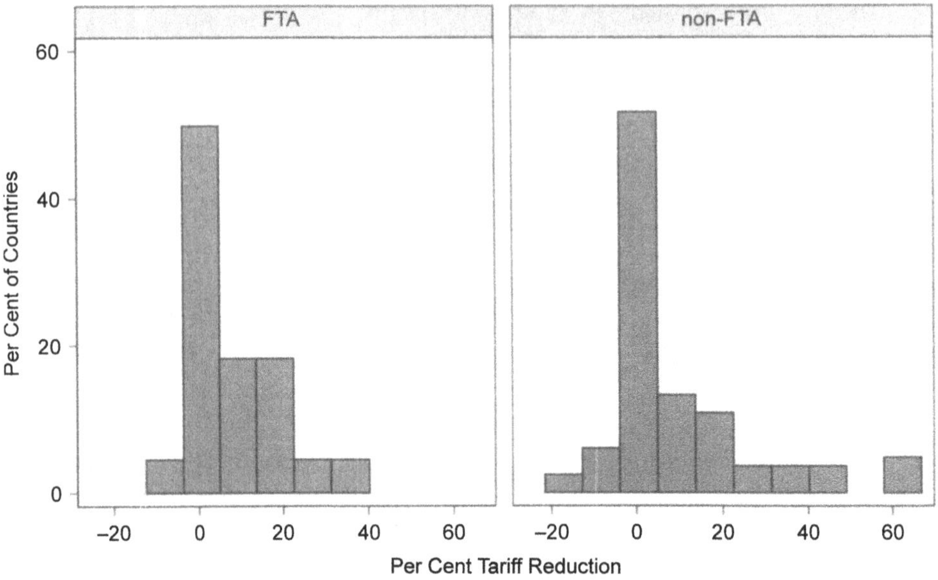

Source: Trends in Applied Average Tariffs: World Bank.

it seems very unlikely that the US FTA selection criterion is based on either post-Uruguay tariff reductions or tariff reductions occurring during the FTA recruitment period.

To be fair, commitment to multilateralism probably involves many factors that are not readily observable *a priori*. Thus, one cannot know for sure if US FTA partners are committed until we witness their liberalisation, or lack thereof, at the completion of the current round of WTO talks. Alternatively, we might be able to infer something from previous cases of countries that implemented FTAs or other preferential arrangements between WTO agreements. Limão (2006) has done this for the US. He looks at changes in US MFN tariffs between the Tokyo and Uruguay Rounds for goods imported from members of US preferential arrangements as compared to goods imported only from non-members. He finds that MFN tariff reductions were significantly smaller on goods in the former category, suggesting a stumbling-block effect of PTAs. Ironically, the focus of debate in the TPR is on whether the commitment to multilateralism of US FTA partners will wane after they join a US FTA, when in fact the best evidence to date suggests it is the US commitment we should be concerned about!

So why is it that US commitment to multilateralism goes unquestioned in the TPR, despite the rash of FTAs? I can think of three reasons: the US reiterates its commitment again and again throughout the TPR, the US has historically been the anchor for the multilateral system and the administrative stumbling-block argument does not fit the US, because the US has more than enough negotiators to conduct both multilateral and bilateral talks. The EU's alternative stumbling-block argument (that bilateral agreements might compromise domestic political support for multilateral liberalisation) fits better, but there is no reason offered for why domestic political support shouldn't just as easily turn in favour of multilateral liberalisation.

But here is where I would like to return to the national security theme. Limão (2006) also makes the argument that FTAs are likely to be stumbling blocks when entered into with small countries for non-economic reasons. The reason is that, if the US grants a small country preferential access to its market in order to obtain something non-economic in exchange – e.g. an ally in its wars against terror or drugs, a stable democratic presence in a troubled region, a strategically important location for military bases, etc. – then neither the US nor its partner will want to see that preferential access eroded by US MFN tariff reductions, as this would defeat the purpose of the deal. Thus, the US will limit its MFN tariff reductions to preserve these preferences. If this argument is correct, then I see a problem.

It would be difficult to argue that the post-2001 US FTAs have been motivated primarily by economic benefits to the United States. While certainly Canada and Mexico are large US trading partners, only three of the more recent US FTA partners individually account for more than one per cent of US total trade. Not including Israel, all of the Middle Eastern FTA partners combined account for less than one per cent. Without Canada and Mexico, the correlation between US FTA membership and volume of trade is virtually zero, which is remarkable because trade volume is endogenous.

On the other hand, the Secretariat's report notes that the US sees open markets as part of a broader global security objective. Numerous countries in the TPR meeting echoed this characterisation. Only the US itself took issue with it, but it is unclear why. The 2002 National Security Strategy (NSS) of the United States makes the point abundantly clear. Indeed, press reports issued by the Office of the US Trade Representative touting the FTAs are quite explicit that they are part of a strategy to bolster moderate regimes in high-risk parts of the world, particularly those in the Middle East and Malaysia.[7] I submit that a good undergraduate research project would be to estimate the probability of membership in a post-2001 US FTA as a function of just two variables: the distance of a country to the nearest al-Qaeda attack, 'rogue state' or narcotics producer, and a dummy

---

[7] 'By solidifying our economic relationship, an FTA with Malaysia will advance other important policy goals, including supporting our partnership on security. Malaysia is a moderate Muslim country in a critical part of the world and has been an important partner in the war on terror', (USTR Fact Sheet on US-Malaysia FTA, March 2006).

variable indicating whether or not the country deployed troops to Iraq in 2003 (that would include Australia, Korea, Singapore, Thailand, El Salvador, Honduras, Nicaragua and the Dominican Republic). I conjecture that these two variables would leave little left to explain.

However, even if I am wrong and US FTAs are being signed utterly at random, there is still the problem that in order to push these agreements through an increasingly protectionist Congress conditions must be attached, particularly labour and (domestic) environmental standards that are unrelated to trade. Bhagwati (2005) summarises the problem as follows:

> But when the United States takes the developing countries, one by one, in a bilateral Free Trade Agreement negotiation, it can exercise hegemonic pressure to get the immensely less powerful partner country to accept almost any 'fair trade' agenda in exchange for a preferential access to its gigantic market. So, the various lobbies in the United States have now shifted from multilateral trade negotiations to bilateral FTAs because they expect a much richer harvest for their own agendas. Thus, every FTA by the U.S. in recent years, while trivial in trade terms, is a milestone for the lobbies who force what are euphemistically called 'WTO plus' obligations as if they represented progress relative to a deficient WTO (p. 11).

This suggests that not only are bilateral deals creating preferences that need to be preserved in order to keep pressure on our partners to live up to the conditions imposed. It also suggests that the bilateral deals are being created precisely because the US is unable to impose these conditions on the WTO more generally.

4. CONCLUSION

The only agreements the US has signed under its trade promotion authority since 2001 have been bilateral and regional deals. There is no evidence that the partners to these deals are any more committed to multilateralism than any other WTO country or that these agreements substantially benefit the US economically. There is ample evidence that the administration's security strategy drives the selection of the partners and that to get these deals past a protectionist Congress further trade-unrelated conditions need to be imposed. Indeed, from this perspective, the US resort to bilateralism appears more as an escape from multilateral disciplines than a 'catalyst to multilateral liberalisation'.

Nonetheless, the US's heightened concern about national security is a fact of life. Indeed, it is a completely appropriate response to the events of 11 September and the continuing threats to its security and that of its allies. The question here is whether an erosion of the multilateral trading system is a necessary consequence. As far as security-related customs procedures and food safety regulations are concerned, additional trade costs are inevitable. The only question for the WTO is whether these measures will mutate into disguised protectionism, which is a problem for sure but one the WTO is capable of addressing. But with respect to bilateralism versus multilateralism, the US has a choice. It is unclear whether the administration has decided that bilateralism is the best way to address its security concerns or simply the only practical way to do so, given the Congressional 'fair trade' agenda. In any event, it strikes me that the threat of terrorism is a global threat, just like the threats faced in WWII and the Cold War. As such, there is no reason why the US should want to support its allies at the expense of its friends. As in earlier days, US trade policy should be directed towards supporting democracy, rule of law and economic development in *all* countries, and the multilateral system is the best tool it has.

REFERENCES

Bhagwati, J. (2005), 'From Seattle to Hong Kong: Are We Getting Anywhere?' (unedited version) *Foreign Affairs* (Special Edition, December, http://www.columbia.edu/~jb38/index_paper01.html).
Busch, M. L. (2007), 'Overlapping Institutions, Forum Shopping and Dispute Settlement in International Trade', *International Organization* (forthcoming, Fall).
Limão, N. (2006), 'Preferential Trade Agreements as Stumbling Blocks for Multilateral Trade Liberalization: Evidence for the United States', *American Economic Review*, **96**, 3, 896–914.

3

Formulating Trade Policy in a Small Hydrocarbon-dependent Economy: The Case of Trinidad and Tobago

Michael Henry

1. INTRODUCTION

THE most recent (2005) WTO *Trade Policy Review* for Trinidad and Tobago (hereafter TPRTT, 2005) contains mixed reviews of that country's trade policy regime for the period 1998–2004. On the one hand, it acknowledges the crucial role trade has played in supporting the country's recent rapid economic growth. Further, it lauds Trinidad and Tobago's commitment to outward-oriented policies and 'to the principle that free trade is the most viable option to achieving social and economic progress'. On the other hand, however, it notes that notwithstanding the country's continued efforts aimed at further liberalising its trade regime, trade policy reforms since the first *Trade Policy Review* in 1998 (TPRTT, 1998), have been 'measured'. For example, although the use of import surcharges (particularly on agricultural imports) has been reduced, the average applied Most Favoured Nation (MFN) tariff remains at 9.1 per cent. Additionally, while non-tariff trade barriers appear to be low, non-automatic licensing is still applied and there has also been an increase in the use of anti-dumping measures. Consequently, TPRTT, 2005, advocates the need for further reforms to eliminate remaining distortions, for example, in the agricultural sector, and deepening of reforms recently initiated in the services sector, particularly in industries like financial services, maritime transport and telecommunications.

In terms of economic performance, TPRTT, 2005, highlights the strong economic growth enjoyed by Trinidad and Tobago over the period 1999–2004 due mainly to high international petroleum prices and other developments in the country's hydrocarbons sector. Over this period, real GDP expanded at an annual average rate of 7.7 per cent, with per capita income increasing to over US$8,000 in 2004. However, the *Report* rightfully laments the fact that the hydrocarbons sector (particularly oil and natural gas) continues to be the mainstay of the country's economy and the seemingly increasing over-reliance of this sector for its economic wellbeing. This undoubtedly makes Trinidad and Tobago vulnerable to large external shocks brought on by large fluctuations in international oil and gas prices. One can also argue that this situation, along with the fact that oil and natural gas are finite non-renewable natural resources, then make diversification of the economy away from hydrocarbons a key imperative to ensure sustainable economic growth and development.

One of the challenges for policy-makers, therefore, becomes the formulation of an appropriate mix of trade and other economic policies to facilitate the development of an internationally competitive non-oil sector that can make a significant contribution to sustainable economic growth. This paper examines the status of Trinidad and Tobago's trade policy regime, as well as other trade-related development factors, based mainly on TPRTT, 2005, and to a lesser extent TPRTT, 1998. In doing so, it highlights the areas identified by the governing body of world trade that the country needs to address to ensure compliance (as far as possible) with the rules, disciplines and commitments made under the Multilateral Trade Agreements; and the existence of a trade policy regime characterised by little or no distortions, thus facilitating a smoother functioning of the global trading system. The paper undertakes this discussion against the background of Trinidad and Tobago's role as a founding member of the regional integration body – CARICOM – and the increasing influence of this body in determining trade and other economic policies adopted by individual member countries. Section 2 sets the stage for the analysis by reviewing Trinidad and Tobago's economic performance and the main elements of its trade regime from the onset of the 1980s up to the country's initiation of unilateral trade and economic reforms towards the end of that decade. Section 3 reviews the trade policy and other macroeconomic reforms undertaken from the beginning of the reform period (1989) to 1998 (the year of the country's first TPR) and the effects of these reforms on economic performance. Section 4 extends the analysis to cover the period 1999 to 2005. Section 5 concludes and discusses the recommendations advanced by the WTO *Report* for broadening the reform process.

2. TRADE POLICY AND ECONOMIC PERFORMANCE 1980–1988: THE PRE-REFORM YEARS

a. Economic Performance

Following a period of rapid economic growth between 1973 and 1982 – triggered by high international oil prices – that led to substantial increases in public sector investment and consumption through the implementation of a resource-based industrialisation (RBI) strategy,[1] Trinidad and Tobago's economy experienced severe economic contraction for most of the 1980s. This resulted in declining output and per capita income; high unemployment; rising current account deficits and loss of foreign exchange reserves. For example, following growth in real GDP of 3.8 per cent in 1982, real output fell sharply by 10.3 per cent the following year; a trend which continued for seven successive years up to 1989 (Table 1). Indeed, during this period (1983–1989) output fell at an average annual rate of 3.7 per cent. Additionally, net foreign reserves declined on average by 3.8 per cent per annum from approximately TT$7.7 billion in 1981 to just over TT$100 million in 1991, while government revenues fell from roughly TT$7.1 billion in 1982 to TT$4.6 billion in 1988 (National Income of Trinidad and Tobago: 1981–1991).

This situation was compounded by the country's increased external indebtedness incurred as a consequence of the RBI strategy pursued. In fact, the deteriorating balance of payments and foreign reserves positions which led to fiscal and external deficits in 1981, culminated in a 48 per cent devaluation of the Trinidad and Tobago dollar – from TT$2.42 = US$1 to TT$3.60 = US$1 – in 1985. A parallel exchange rate regime also existed whereby food, drugs and agricultural inputs were subjected to the old exchange rate. However, in August of 1988 this regime was eliminated when the dollar was further devalued to TT$4.25 = US$1.

This sudden reversal in the country's economic fortunes was precipitated by the dramatic fall in both international oil prices and domestic crude oil production in the post-1982 period. For instance, petroleum prices which peaked at US$33.47 per barrel in 1982, fell to US$29.31 per barrel in 1983; the first fall since the initial oil shock of the last quarter of 1973. The situation worsened when prices plummeted to US$15 per barrel in 1986. On the other hand, domestic production of crude oil, which peaked at 83.8 million barrels in 1978, fell at an average annual rate of 3.5 per cent to 53 million barrels in 1991 (*National Income of Trinidad and Tobago: 1981–1991*).

Faced with economic crisis, the country unilaterally implemented measures aimed at both stabilising and restructuring the economy. Between 1983 and 1986, these measures mainly took the form of expenditure reduction. Thus efforts were made to streamline public expenditure and the incentive structure of the private sector changed. This included, among other things, freezing wages and salaries of public sector employees at 1982 levels, the reduction of subsidies on gasoline and basic foodstuffs, and imposition of indirect taxes on a wide range of locally produced and imported goods.

---

[1] Available figures show that in 1982 public sector gross capital formation was 58.5 per cent of total capital formation while in 1985 it was approximately 50 per cent. Additionally, the share of persons classified as government employees rose from approximately 18 per cent between the 1960s to the early 1970s, to over 30 per cent in the 1980s (*Republic of Trinidad and Tobago National Income Report 1981–91*; and Harrison, 2002).

MICHAEL HENRY

TABLE 1

Trinidad and Tobago: Selected Economic Indicators 1980–1988

	1980	1981	1982	1983	1984	1985	1986	1987	1988
Real GDP Growth (Per cent)	10.4	4.6	3.8	-10.3	-5.8	-4.1	-3.3	-4.6	-3.9
Fiscal Operations									
Tot. Govt. Revenue (TT $M)	6,081.6	6,988.9	7,046.4	6,518.8	6,502.9	6,439.1	5,186.5	5,154.2	4,657.2
Tot. Govt. Expenditure (TT $M)	3,448.8	3,853.9	6,323.0	6,445.7	6,208.4	6,119.7	5,791.9	5,532.8	5,118.0
Overall Surplus/Deficit (TT $M)	2,632.8	3,135.0	723.4	73.1	294.5	319.4	-605.4	-378.6	-460.8
Unemployment Rate (Per cent)	10.0	10.2	10.0	11.0		15.7	17.2	22.3	22.0

Source: *The National Income of Trinidad and Tobago*, various years; *Review of the Economy* (1994; 1998–99); and *World Development Indicators* (World Bank).

The year 1987 saw a new government in power and with it intensification of the adjustment process through a medium-term adjustment programme, aimed at stimulating exports, reducing imports via rigid foreign exchange controls, and encouraging investment (domestic and foreign) through the use of fiscal incentives. There was also a continuation of the policy of expenditure reduction, with cuts in salaries of public officers, a significant reduction in transfers and subsidies to state enterprises and public utilities, a ban on garment imports other than for personal use and a further tightening of exchange controls. This was followed by a currency devaluation in 1988 and tightening of liquidity along with other restrictive financial and monetary policies.[2]

b. Trade Policy Framework

At the start of the 1980s, the trade policy regime which offered protection to domestic industry in the non-oil manufacturing sector during the oil boom years was still largely maintained. This inward-oriented trade regime was characterised by high tariff and non-tariff barriers (NTBs) and other restrictive policies; a relic of the import-substituting industrialisation (ISI) development strategy pursued at the onset of the 1970s. As indicated above, the trade regime became even more restrictive in the post-1982 period. However, Asad and Rajapatirana (1993) argue that while some Latin American and Caribbean (LAC) countries raised their trade barriers during the 1980s in an effort to respond to balance-of-payments crises, these barriers reinforced, in varying degrees, the inward orientation that characterised their trade policies for much of the postwar era.

Although data on many of the measures prevailing are sparse, there is a fair amount of anecdotal evidence of high and variable tariff rates; foreign exchange restrictions; pervasive and stringent quantitative restrictions (QRs) and discretionary licensing of imports; many discretionary exceptions both as to who gets protection and who gets special treatment; and export taxes (see Asad and Rajapatirana, 1993; and Finger et al., 1998). For example, according to UNECLAC (1999) the CARICOM Common External Tariff (CET), together with a host of other NTBs, was highly protective. Further, tariffs were said to be highly dispersed with 16 tariff rates ranging from 0 to 70 per cent but with over nine-tenths of the tariff positions at or below 45 per cent. Asad and Rajapatirana (1993) present data on Trinidad and Tobago for 1991 which showed an average unweighted legal tariff rate (including tariff surcharges) of 41 per cent and a tariff range of 0–103 per cent for that country. These figures were largely corroborated by Finger et al. (1998) who also noted the existence of import licences for consumer

---

[2] These included *inter alia* reduced growth rate of money supply; restriction of credit to state enterprises; increases in the statutory reserve requirement that commercial banks are required to hold; and an increase in the rediscount rate.

goods, while many goods were either banned or subjected to QRs. Further, state trading enterprises (STEs) existed for rice, wheat, fats and oils, and petroleum.

Towards the end of the review period, however, more and more measures aimed at liberalising trade were being implemented. For example, there was a dismantling of the negative list which in 1988 saw 40 per cent of the items removed (Harrison, 2002). Among the factors that prompted the shift in policy were, first, an international environment that increasingly favoured liberal trade policies and, second, the juxtaposition of the extraordinary success of the strongly export-oriented East Asian newly industrialised economies (NIEs) with the poor economic performance of inward-oriented developing countries (see *World Development Report*, 1987; Greenaway and Nam, 1988; and Greenaway et al., 2002).

The reforms had differing effects on both the average levels and growth rates of imports and exports. Whereas the level of imports declined for all years between 1982 and 1989 (with the exception of 1986), generally there was an upward trend in real exports while real imports declined on average by 1.9 per cent between 1981 and 1991, real exports grew on average by 2.8 per cent (*National Accounts of Trinidad and Tobago: 1981–1991*). In terms of the composition of exports, the share of crude petroleum in total exports fell from 72 per cent in 1981 to 55 per cent in 1991. In contrast, significant growth was recorded by the non-oil sector which in 1991 accounted for 28 per cent of total exports compared to 11 per cent in 1981. This growth was led by petrochemicals, iron and steel, and manufactured goods. Steady growth was also recorded in exports of non-factor services from 1988 to 1991.

3. TRADE POLICY AND ECONOMIC PERFORMANCE 1989–1998: THE REFORM YEARS

Although Trinidad and Tobago's programme of structural adjustment began before 1989, its 'official' IMF and World Bank Programme began in 1988/1989. Although the short-term goals of both programmes were essentially the same, there were two key differences between them. First, with the 'official' programme there were fewer opportunities for policy reversals by the authorities in the face of unintended consequences of the measures. Second, trade policy reforms (particularly for imports) had a much greater role in the 'official' programme.

The initial period of the structural adjustment programme was supported by two Stand-by Arrangements with the IMF in January of 1989 and April of 1990, together with a Structural Adjustment Loan from the World Bank.

a. Economic Performance

The first five-year period following the 'official' start of the adjustment programme saw the continued implementation of policies aimed at reducing government expenditure; finding an appropriate exchange rate regime; liberalising trade; and monetary and financial policies aimed at stabilising the level of foreign reserves. Following the cutting of public sector workers' cost-of-living allowances and merit increases in 1987, salaries were further cut by 10 per cent in 1989 and subsidies and transfers to state enterprises and public utilities were significantly reduced. These measures were implemented in conjunction with complementary monetary and financial policies aimed at tightening liquidity. Two key measures were restrictions of the money supply and movement towards positive real interest rates. A comprehensive tax reform programme was also embarked upon which led to changes in individual income taxation and the imposition of a system of value-added taxation (VAT) at a rate of 15 per cent on a wide range of commodities.

In 1990, after seven successive years of economic contraction, the economy recorded growth in real GDP of 1.5 per cent (Table 2), and 2.7 per cent in 1991. Notwithstanding the change in government at the end of 1991, the adjustment process continued unchecked. A devaluation of approximately 35 per cent, together with the introduction of a managed floating exchange rate regime in 1993, were implemented early in the life of the new government. However, on account of the declines experienced in petroleum output in 1992 and 1993, there was a corresponding fall in the growth of real GDP of 1.7 and 1.4 per cent respectively in those two years and the rate of unemployment remained high, averaging around 18 per cent for the period 1991–1994.

Between 1994 and 1998, growth accelerated to over three per cent per year largely due to the petroleum sector – particularly petrochemicals – but also due to growth in the non-oil sector. Manufacturing output grew appreciably as the effects of trade and investment liberalisation began to take hold. During this period there was also a downward trend in both inflation and unemployment, the former falling from 8.8 per cent in 1994 to 5.6 per cent in 1998, while the latter fell from 18.4 to 14.2 per cent over the same period. Moreover, as a result of improvements in tax collection, proceeds from privatisation, and reductions in government subsidies and transfers, the central government posted budget surpluses from 1995, reaching 1.7 per cent of GDP in 1997 after which a deficit was once again incurred in 1998 (TPRTT, 1998).

In contrast, the trade surplus that Trinidad and Tobago enjoyed throughout the first half of the 1990s fell over the entire 1994–1998 period, with deficits being recorded in the last two years of the period as imports grew faster than exports. In fact, while the former more than doubled between 1993 and 1997, the latter increased by only 50 per cent. This was fuelled by the rapid increases in consumer and capital goods demand and currency appreciation (TPRTT, 1998; and *Republic of Trinidad and Tobago: Review of the Economy, 1998–1999*).

Another significant development was the sharp rise in inflows of foreign direct investment (FDI). Trinidad and Tobago is the leading English-speaking

TABLE 2
Trinidad and Tobago: Selected Economic Indicators 1989–1998

	1989	1990	1991	1992	1993	1994	1995	1996	1997	1998
Real GDP Growth (Per cent)	−0.8	1.5	2.7	−1.7	−1.5	3.6	4.0	3.8	3.1	4.4
Inflation (CPI, Per cent)	11.4	11.0	3.8	6.5	10.8	8.8	5.3	3.3	3.6	5.6
Fiscal Operations										
Tot. Govt. Revenue (TT $M)	4,878.2	5,622.7	6,757.7	6,101.3	6,744.2	7,565.3	8,511.6	9,542.5	10,453.7	10,615.5
Tot. Govt. Expenditure (TT $M)	5,642.0	5,891.1	6,803.6	6,745.1	6,783.3	7,571.3	8,458.3	9,371.5	10,412.3	11,596.7
Overall Surplus/Deficit (TT $M)	−763.8	−268.4	−45.9	−643.8	−39.1	−6.0	53.3	171.0	41.4	−981.2
Gross Foreign Reserves (US $M)	378.0	581.8	426.9	316.1	446.0	678.9	652.3	937.7	1,120.3	1,184.5
Unemployment Rate (Per cent)	22.0	20.0	18.5	19.6	19.8	18.4	17.2	16.2	15.0	14.2

Source: *The National Income of Trinidad and Tobago*, various years; *Review of the Economy* (1994; 1998–99); *Annual Economic Survey, 2005*; and WTO, *Trade Policy Review of Trinidad and Tobago 2005*.

Caribbean country in attracting FDI. In 1997 and 1998, the country accounted for approximately 60 per cent and 50 per cent, respectively, of the approximately US$1.6 billion of FDI inflows to the region (TPRTT, 1998). Most of the inflows (approximately 80 per cent) went to the petroleum and petrochemical sectors with the US being the single largest foreign investor.

The above development can, in no small measure, be attributed to the steps taken by government to liberalise its investment regime to make the business climate more investor friendly. Measures included the granting of fiscal and other incentives; legal and other regulatory amendments (for example, the repealing of legislation which previously prevented foreigners from owning property such as land and buildings); being a signatory of many bilateral investment treaties (BITS) and double-taxation treaties for the protection of foreign capital; the provision of a stable macroeconomic climate (e.g. stable exchange rates); ensuring application of the rule of law and protection of property rights; and improvements of the physical and social infrastructure.

b. Trade Policy Reforms[3]

Among the notable measures to further liberalise trade were removal – in the second quarter of 1992 – of most of the items on the negative list; elimination and/or tariffication of NTBs such as QRs; the virtual dismantling of price controls and reduction of import duties under CARICOM provisions (see Harrison, 2002; and TPRTT, 1998). On the export side there was a reduction or elimination of price and quantitative barriers to exports and introduction or improvement of measures for export promotion and diversification.

Additionally, the role of the private sector in economic activity was greatly enhanced through an incentive structure designed to create a more competitive private sector to stimulate private investment and exports and facilitate the movement towards trade liberalisation. These were undertaken mainly through monetary, financial and trade policies and included exchange rate devaluation; trade liberalisation to remove the barriers to trade; disbanding of import restrictions; and tax reforms.

Trinidad and Tobago (a GATT contracting party since October, 1962), became a WTO Member in March, 1995. As a result of the Uruguay Round, most industrial tariffs were bound at a ceiling of 50 per cent. Some products, however, were bound at 70 per cent.[4] There was a substantial gap between bound rates and applied tariffs which peaked at 30 per cent. All agricultural lines were bound

---

[3] This sub-section draws heavily (though not exclusively) on the WTO's *Trade Policy Review of Trinidad and Tobago 1998.*

[4] These included table salt, Portland cement, some cosmetics, paper products, garments (all of HS Chapters 61 and 62), footwear, some household durables, cars and car parts.

mostly at 100 per cent while other duties and charges were bound at 15 per cent. Most final bound rates were implemented in a one-step process in 1995.

Post-1990 the regional integration process in the Caribbean continued to deepen in response to developments in the global multilateral trading system, particularly as they (the developments) relate to the African, Caribbean and Pacific (ACP) group of developing countries (e.g. the dismantling of preferential trading arrangements). Thus Trinidad and Tobago adopted CARICOM's Common External Tariff (CET) in 1991[5] and implemented the four-phase schedule of CET reductions between 1995 and 1 July, 1998, with the maximum import duties for industrial products being lowered from 35 to 20 per cent in four phases.

In contrast, the maximum applied rates for agricultural goods remained at 40 per cent over the whole of the implementation period. This notwithstanding, the reductions meant that by 1998 Trinidad and Tobago's unweighted average MFN tariff had declined to 9.1 per cent. Nominal protection on agricultural products was much higher with an average rate of 19.1 per cent, while industrial imports were subjected to an average tariff of seven per cent.

Tariff rates imposed under the CET depend on the nature of the taxable commodity. Most commodities are grouped as either competing (if regional production satisfies at least 75 per cent of regional demand) or non-competing. Each group is then subdivided into inputs (primary, intermediate and capital) and final goods. The rate structure is 0 or 5 per cent on non-competing inputs; 10 per cent on competing primary and capital inputs; 15 per cent on competing intermediate inputs; and 20 per cent on all final goods. Additionally, the CET agreement allows for a special rate on agricultural products, limited duty exemptions related to economic development, and some additional national discretion in the setting of tariff rates (Stotsky et al., 2000).

Despite the progress made, the agricultural sector continued to be heavily protected and in fact is the country's most heavily protected sector. Agriculture, together with food processing, beverages and tobacco contribute slightly more than five per cent of GDP but employ about 14 per cent of the labour force. In the Uruguay Round, Trinidad and Tobago bound its tariffs on all agricultural products at ceiling rates of 100 per cent with the exception of seven items which were bound at higher levels.[6] During this period, applied tariffs on agricultural products varied between 0 and 40 per cent. As indicated above, in 1998, the simple average

---

[5] The CET were adopted for all goods except for a group of mainly agricultural products (List A) and industrial goods (List C).

[6] These products are poultry not cut in pieces, fresh or chilled (HS 020710); fatty livers of geese or ducks, fresh/chilled (HS 020731); poultry cuts and offal other than fatty livers, fresh or chilled (HS 020739); cuts of fowl of the species *Gallus Domesticus*, frozen (HS 020741), all bound at a base rate of 135 per cent, and at 110 per cent as of 2005; and cabbage, fresh (HS 0704001), bound at 126 per cent; lettuce, fresh (HS 070510), bound at 156 per cent; and coffee, roasted coffee beans (HS 090120), bound at 106 per cent, all as of 2005 (see TPRTT, 2005).

MFN tariff on agricultural products was 19.1 per cent. In addition some agricultural products also incurred high levels of import surcharges, for example poultry (100 per cent), sugar and icing sugar (60–75 per cent), vegetables (15 per cent) and fruit (five per cent). Under a schedule established in 1995, surcharges on bovine meat and milk were to be eliminated by 1998, while those on fruits and vegetables were to be removed by 1999. Surcharges on poultry parts were to be reduced in 2004. However, surcharges on sugar (60 per cent), icing sugar (75 per cent) and on some poultry products (86 per cent) were not subject to reduction.

Incentives given to the agricultural sector included subsidies for soil conservation, equipment and machinery, agricultural vehicles and wheel tractors, as well as price support for sugarcane, coffee, cocoa, milk, oranges, grapefruit, paddy, copra and sorrel. Payments granted for price support totalled approximately TT$36 million in 1997 while input subsidies totalled TT$0.4 million. Taken together, these payments accounted for some 1.8 per cent of agricultural GDP (TPRTT, 1998). Meanwhile, import duties on alcoholic beverages were set at specific rates, ranging from TT$4.75 per litre for beer to TT$40.00 per litre for cordials and liqueurs. With respect to alcoholic beverages that are produced locally and regionally, these are subject to excise duties.

Despite the protection and fiscal support given to the agricultural sector, its performance over the period continued to be disappointing with its share of GDP declining from 2.4 per cent in 1988–1994 to 2.2 per cent in 1995–1998. Similarly, the growth of agricultural output fell from an average of 4.3 per cent between 1988 and 1994, to –4.5 per cent between 1995 and 1998.

By contrast, the rate of growth in manufacturing output rose significantly towards the end of the review period. The sector, however, continues to be heavily dependent on oil refining and petrochemicals. In fact, petroleum-related manufacturing accounts for two-thirds of total manufacturing GDP. The 1998 average MFN tariff on imports of industrial products was seven per cent, with a peak of 30 per cent and minimum rate of zero. The highest tariffs were on arms and ammunition, clocks and watches, works of art, clothing and apparel articles, carpets, furniture, toys, footwear, soap and leather goods. Further, a number of incentive schemes are available to manufacturers. Customs duty concessions are granted to imports of machinery, equipment and materials for a wide range of approved manufacturing activities. Relief from corporation tax and customs duty is granted to approved enterprises for a period of up to 10 years.

Initiatives undertaken in the services sector represents another progressive aspect of liberalisation. This sector, which accounts for over 60 per cent of GDP and 75 per cent of total employment, has been largely liberalised with market access being fairly open in most sub-sectors. Specific commitments were made under the GATS on several service industries including tourism, business, transport and financial services. Additionally, the country participated in and presented offers in the subsequent WTO negotiations on telecommunications and financial services.

With respect to exports, Trinidad and Tobago applies no export taxes. However, the country maintains a system of export licensing for some products, mainly for security and health purposes but also for the purpose of controlling the re-export of capital goods imported under preferential conditions. There are no export quotas, except those determined under bilateral arrangements, nor specific export performance requirements.

Finally, since becoming a member of the WTO, Trinidad and Tobago has amended several pieces of domestic legislation to comply with its obligations under the WTO. These included anti-dumping legislation and regulations to conform to the WTO Anti-dumping Agreement; adoption of new Patent and Copyright Acts and amendment of legislation regarding trademarks and industrial designs to conform to the TRIPS Agreement. Additionally, legislation with respect to trade secrets and unfair competition were put in place.

4. TRADE POLICY AND ECONOMIC PERFORMANCE 1999–2005: A PERIOD OF SUSTAINED AND RISING ECONOMIC GROWTH

Over the period 1999–2005, and continuing to the present, Trinidad and Tobago once again experienced an economic windfall on account of rising oil prices, record high commodity prices and the ongoing expansion of its domestic energy sector. From all indications, the current boom is bigger than the one the country experienced from 1974–1982. To illustrate, St. Cyr (2007) notes that in the last fiscal year (2005/6) government revenue amounted to TT$38 billion, whereas in the 10 years, 1974–1983, total revenue was TT$38 billion! As a consequence, the country has enjoyed robust economic growth since 1994.

As highlighted in TPRTT, 2005, between 1999 and 2004, Trinidad and Tobago's average annual economic growth of 7.7 per cent was twice that of the global economy (3.8 per cent). This was accompanied by other favourable macroeconomic developments such as a declining unemployment rate, low levels of inflation (though rising appreciably in the post-2005 period), record levels of FDI inflows and a strengthening of the overall balance of payments. The upshot of these developments has been a significant reduction in Trinidad and Tobago's domestic and external resource constraints. In terms of its trade policy, the measures undertaken were largely one of consolidation of initiatives taken prior to 1998 rather than the initiation of a host of new measures aimed at broadening the trade policy matrix.

a. Economic Performance

At the end of 2005, the country had experienced its 12th consecutive year of economic growth with the economy growing at an average annual rate of 8.5 per cent between 1999 and 2005 (Table 3),[7] and provisional estimates put the rate of growth for 2006 at an astounding 12 per cent. This was the primary driver of the substantial increase in per capita income from just over US$5,400 in 1999 to an estimated US$11,000 in 2005. The engine of this growth is the strong performance of the energy sector: hydrocarbons real GDP expanding at an annual average of 14.7 per cent between 1999 and 2005, with growth in the non-hydrocarbons sector at an average annual growth rate of 4.7 per cent over the corresponding period. The main drivers of growth in the non-energy sector were the manufacturing and construction sectors; the latter being the beneficiary of government's major infrastructural development and housing thrust, as well as robust private sector construction activity.

On the back of the economic windfall the central government has been able to achieve both current and overall surpluses in its fiscal operations. These accrued despite a marked increase in government expenditure. For example, although expenditure grew by 27.6 per cent for fiscal year 2005, the government posted a surplus of TT$4.6 billion or 5.1 per cent of GDP. This was more than three times the surplus posted in the previous fiscal year.[8] A significant development over the period was the establishment of a Revenue Stabilisation Fund in 2000, where government deposits surplus revenues from the petroleum sector when prices exceed a determined base price. The Fund is intended to act as a buffer against any unexpected drop in petroleum prices as well as strengthen the public sector savings effort. As a result of the surpluses accruing to the government it was able to increase the balance of the Fund, which at the end of fiscal year 2005 had an accumulated balance of TT$5.2 billion.

Other positive aspects of the country's macroeconomic performance included a downward trending rate of unemployment over the entire period. Indeed, eight per cent in 2005 represented Trinidad and Tobago's lowest rate in the past 20 years. The provisional estimate for 2006 puts the figure even lower at 6.8 per cent.

The balance of payments position also strengthened significantly: the current account surplus rose from 0.4 per cent of GDP in 1999, to an estimated 18.5 per cent of GDP in 2005, due mainly to higher petroleum prices and increased natural gas exports. Between 1999 and 2005, exports increased by 214 per cent to reach a record US$8.8 billion in 2005. In addition, Trinidad and Tobago continued to receive record levels of FDI – approximately US$700 million annually and almost US$1 billion in 2004 – in contrast to the declining inflows going to the Americas. Its external reserves position was also strengthened,

---

[7] Unless otherwise stated, the figures presented in this section are taken from the *Trade Policy Review of Trinidad and Tobago 2005* (WTO); *Annual Economic Survey 2005* (Central Bank of Trinidad and Tobago); *Review of the Economy 2006* (Ministry of Finance); and *The National Income of Trinidad and Tobago*, various issues (Central Statistical Office).

[8] The Fiscal Year is the 12-month period from 1 October to September 30.

TABLE 3
Trinidad and Tobago: Selected Economic Indicators 1999–2005

	1999	2000	2001	2002	2003	2004	2005
Real GDP Growth (Per cent)	8.8	7.3	4.2	7.9	14.4	8.8	8.0
Fiscal Operations							
Tot. Govt. Revenue (TT $M)	10,429.3	12,164.7	14,381.0	14,122.5	17,366.6	20,885.4	29,674.8
Tot. Govt. Expenditure (TT $M)	10,484.3	12,460.2	13,990.9	14,226.8	16,591.6	20,673.9	27,234.0
Overall Surplus/Deficit (TT $M)	−55.0	−295.5	390.1	−104.3	775.0	211.5	2,413.8
Gross Foreign Reserves (US $M)	964.0	1,405.0	1,876.0	1,923.6	2,257.8	2,993.0	4,885.7
Inflation (CPI, Per cent)	3.4	3.8	5.6	4.2	3.8	3.7	6.9
Unemployment Rate (Per cent)	13.1	12.1	10.8	10.4	10.5	8.3	8.0[P]

Note:
P: Provisional.

Source: *The National Income of Trinidad and Tobago*, various years; *Review of the Economy* (1994; 1998–99); *Annual Economic Survey 2005*; and WTO, *Trade Policy Review of Trinidad and Tobago 2005*.

increasing more than fivefold from around US$945 million (or 3.1 months of import cover) in 1999 to US$4.9 billion (or 9.7 months of import cover) in 2005. Further, the exchange rate which is *de facto* pegged to the US dollar remained steady during the period.

For most of the review period, inflation had been kept in check, the annual average between 1999 and 2004 being 4.2 per cent. However, triggered by high food prices, inflationary pressures began to build up towards the end of the period. This was compounded by rapid growth in domestic demand coupled with the emergence of domestic supply-side bottlenecks. Together, these two factors prompted a significant rise in merchandise imports that added to the inflationary pressures. As a result, headline inflation averaged 6.9 per cent (7.2 per cent on an end-of-year basis) in 2005 as the increase in food prices reached 22.6 per cent.

Notwithstanding the trade policies and incentive schemes used to promote other activities, Trinidad and Tobago's reliance on the hydrocarbons has increased since 1998. This sector directly generates over one-third of GDP and two-thirds of merchandise exports. Further, activities like steel production and electricity generation are largely dependent on it. The contribution of manufacturing to real GDP remained fairly constant over the period with an annual share of approximately seven per cent. In contrast, the share of agriculture trended downward and accounted for only 0.7 per cent of GDP in 2005. In fact, between 2003 and 2005, output from the agricultural sector fell by an average annual rate of 10.3 per cent, despite high levels of trade protection and fiscal incentives.

Similarly, the contribution of the services sector declined (albeit slightly) over the review period to average roughly about 54 per cent for each of the years between 2003 and 2005. This partly reflected the increased share of hydrocarbons in GDP. Towards the end of the period the largest contributor to GDP from this sector was financial services, followed by distribution.

b. Trade Policy Measures: 1999–2005[9]

Trinidad and Tobago's trade policy measures over 1999–2005 can best be described as one of consolidation of the reform process of the mid-1990s rather than a fundamental broadening of that process. The measures employed largely involved the reduction and/or elimination of tariffs, surcharges and other duties; strengthening of the legal and regulatory framework to bring domestic legislation in conformity with the TRIPS Agreement; and the continuation of initiatives aimed at liberalising the services sector particularly with respect to financial services and telecommunications.

---

[9] The trade policy analysis undertaken in this section is primarily based on the WTO's *Trade Policy Review of Trinidad and Tobago 2005*.

(i) Trade policy instruments and other measures affecting imports

At 1 January, 2004, Trinidad and Tobago's customs tariffs comprised 6,437 tariff lines at the eight-digit level (Table 4). Nearly all of the rates were *ad valorem*. Specific duties were applied to just 27 tariff lines. There were 11 'permanent' tiers with rates ranging from 0 to 45 per cent. However, in 2004, as a result of temporary orders, a few products were subjected to rates of 50 and 60 per cent respectively.

For the period under review, there had been little or no change in Trinidad and Tobago's average applied MFN tariff since the country's first Trade Policy Review in 1998; the figure in 2004 (9.1 per cent, excluding specific duties) being exactly the same as it was in 1998. When tariff surcharges are included, the figure rises to 9.2 per cent. In terms of product types, the level of tariff protection for agricultural products is significantly higher than for non-agricultural (industrial) goods: 17.1 per cent (17.9 per cent inclusive of surcharges) for the former compared to 7.6 per cent for the latter (Table 5). The corresponding figures for 1998 were 19.1 and seven per cent respectively. Additionally, whereas duty-free rates in the agricultural sector concern only 6.1 per cent of the tariff lines, for the industrial sector it is 38.9 per cent. Further, while 44 per cent of the lines in the agricultural sector have rates less than or equal to 10 per cent, the share reaches 69 per cent for non-agricultural products. In fact, more than two-thirds of non-agricultural products face rates less than or equal to five per cent.

In a continuation of the trend started in the 1990s, the period saw a decline in the importance of tariffs as a source of government revenue. For example, in fiscal year 2003–4, revenue accruing from customs duties was estimated to be TT$1 billion (US$160 million). This amounted to 4.7 per cent of total government

TABLE 4
Tariff Structure of Trinidad and Tobago, 2004
(Number of lines and per cent)

1.	Total number of tariff lines	6,437
2.	Non-*ad valorem* tariffs (Per cent of all tariff lines)	0.4
3.	Non-*ad valorem* with no AVEs (Per cent of all tariff lines)	0.4
4.	Tariff quotas (Per cent of all tariff lines)	0.0
5.	Duty-free tariff lines (Per cent of all tariff lines)	45.4
6.	Dutiable lines tariff average rate (Per cent)	16.7
7.	Domestic tariff 'peaks' (Per cent of all tariff lines)[a]	8.4
8.	International tariff 'peaks' (Per cent of all tariff lines)[b]	28.2
9.	Bound tariff lines (Per cent of all tariff lines)	100.0

Notes:
Calculations are done by the WTO Secretariat based on data provided by the authorities of Trinidad and Tobago.
[a] Domestic tariff peaks are defined as those exceeding three times the overall average applied rate.
[b] International tariff peaks are defined as those exceeding 15 per cent.

Source: WTO, *Trade Policy Review of Trinidad and Tobago 2005* (Table III.2).

TABLE 5
Summary Analysis of Trinidad and Tobago's MFN Tariff, 2004

Description	MFN				Final Bound
	No. of Lines	Average (Per cent)	Range (Per cent)	Coefficient of Variation (CV)	Average[a] (Per cent)
Total	**6,437**	**9.1**	**0–60**	**1.3**	**57.2**
HS 01–24	1,128	19.7	0–60	0.9	85.1
HS 25–97	5,309	6.9	0–60	1.3	51.3
By WTO Category					
WTO Agriculture	1,052	17.1	0–60	1.0	89.9
Animals and products thereof	151	22.9	0–40	0.7	84.6
Dairy products	24	12.5	0–40	1.1	100.0
Coffee and tea, cocoa, sugar etc.	170	17.2	0–60	0.9	94.3
Cut flowers, plants	56	7.5	0–40	2.0	73.9
Fruit and vegetables	259	23.8	0–40	0.7	96.7
Grains	29	14.5	0–40	0.9	76.4
Oil seeds, fats and oils and their products	96	15.7	0–40	1.2	88.0
Beverages and spirits	108	21.1	0–40	0.6	100.0
Tobacco	10	21.0	0–30	0.7	100.0
Other agricultural products n.e.s.	149	2.5	0–40	2.9	81.3
WTO Non-agriculture (incl. petroleum)	5,385	7.6	0–60	1.3	50.8
WTO Non-agriculture (excl. petroleum)	5,359	7.6	0–60	1.3	50.8
Fish and fishery products	162	26.6	0–40	0.6	50.6
Mineral products, precious stones and metals	398	8.7	0–60	1.2	43.6
Metals	729	5.1	0–20	1.2	47.8
Chemicals and photographic supplies	1,021	4.0	0–25	1.7	50.6
Leather, rubber, footwear and travel goods	184	8.2	0–30	1.1	50.9
Wood, pulp, paper and furniture	321	7.1	0–20	1.2	50.5
Textile and clothing	975	9.0	0–30	1.1	56.9
Transport equipment	187	8.6	0–45	1.3	52.6
Non-electric machinery	591	3.1	0–30	2.2	50.3
Electric machinery	266	9.1	0–50	0.9	53.1
Non-agriculture articles n.e.s.	525	12.3	0–30	0.8	49.2
Petroleum	26	11.0	0–30	1.3	45.6
By ISIC Sector[b]					
Agriculture and fisheries	429	20.6	0–40	0.9	66.7
Mining	114	3.2	0–30	2.7	38.4
Manufacturing	5,893	8.4	0–60	1.3	56.8

TABLE 5 *Continued*

Description	MFN				Final Bound Averageª (Per cent)
	No. of Lines	Average (Per cent)	Range (Per cent)	Coefficient of Variation (CV)	
By HS Section					
01 Live animals & prod.	320	24.2	0–40	0.7	71.6
02 Vegetable products	400	18.0	0–40	1.1	84.3
03 Fats & oils	53	25.3	0–40	0.7	97.0
04 Prepared food etc.	355	16.4	0–60	0.7	96.9
05 Minerals	191	4.9	0–60	2.0	41.9
06 Chemical & prod.	959	3.5	0–25	1.9	51.8
07 Plastics & rubber	245	6.9	0–30	1.1	52.1
08 Hides & skins	84	7.2	0–20	1.3	46.3
09 Wood & articles	124	7.4	0–20	1.1	45.9
10 Pulp, paper etc.	172	5.3	0–20	1.5	50.9
11 Textile & articles	962	8.5	0–20	1.1	57.4
12 Footwear, headgear	66	15.5	0–20	0.5	59.7
13 Articles of stone	182	10.0	0–25	0.8	46.7
14 Precious stones, etc.	62	15.6	0–30	1.0	44.3
15 Base metals & prod.	721	5.6	0–20	1.2	48.5
16 Machinery	890	5.4	0–50	1.5	51.4
17 Transport equipment	198	8.4	0–45	1.3	52.5
18 Precision equipment	249	9.7	0–30	1.1	48.3
19 Arms and ammunition	24	21.6	0–30	0.5	41.0
20 Miscellaneous manufacturing	172	15.0	0–20	0.4	52.4
21 Works of art, etc.	8	20.0	0–20	0.0	50.0
By Stage of Processing					
First stage of processing	845	15.3	0–40	1.2	62.4
Semi-processed products	1,890	2.1	0–60	2.6	50.8
Fully-processed products	3,702	11.2	0–60	0.9	59.1

Notes:
Calculations are done by the WTO Secretariat based on data provided by the authorities of Trinidad and Tobago.
ª Bound rates are not provided in the same HS classification as MFN rates. Therefore the number of lines may not be the same or correspond between the two series.
ᵇ ISIC (Rev.2) classification, excluding electricity (1 line).

Source: WTO, *Trade Policy Review of Trinidad and Tobago 2005*, Table III.3.

revenue, a decline from the 5.2 per cent that was reported in TPRTT, 1998. Indeed, the declining share of trade taxes in government revenues has been a feature of many developing countries in the last decade or so. Customs duties represented approximately 3.8 per cent of the value of imports in 2003.

Since 1998, tariff dispersion – measured by the coefficient of variation – has remained fairly constant. About 45.4 per cent of all tariff lines are duty free while a similar proportion (45 per cent) are subject to rates ranging from 2.5 to 20 per cent. A further 6.3 per cent of lines carry rates higher than 30 per cent (see Figure 1). Further, domestic tariff peaks, which are over three times the average value, account for 8.4 per cent of all tariff lines, and mainly affect agricultural products.

However, TPRTT, 2005, points to some evidence that Trinidad and Tobago's current tariff structure is characterised by tariff escalation with the average tariff applied to fully processed goods being substantially higher than for semi-processed products.

Specific duties are applied to alcoholic beverages and film (27 lines); products included in List C of the CET Exceptions (Table 6). Two likely consequences of these duties on alcoholic beverages are that they can result in relatively high

FIGURE 1
Frequency Distribution of MFN Tariff Rates, 2004

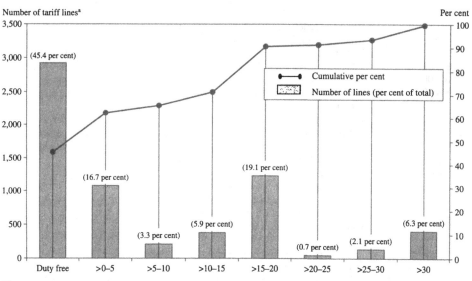

Note:
WTO Secretariat calculations, based on data provided by the authorities of Trinidad and Tobago.
[a] The total number of lines is 6,437. Due to the non-use of some of the non-*ad valorem* duties in the calculations, the figures may not sum to 100 per cent.

Source: WTO, *Trade Policy Review of Trinidad and Tobago 2005*, Chart III.1.

TABLE 6
Specific Duties, 2004

HS Heading	Product Description	Specific Duty Rate
22030010	Beer	$5.20 per litre
22030020	Stout	$6.50 per litre
22030090	Other beer made from malt	$6.50 per litre
22041000	Sparkling wine	$52.00 per litre
22042100	Other wine, in containers holding two litres or less	$28.75 per litre
22051000	Vermouth, in containers holding two litres or less	$39.00 per litre
22059000	Vermouth, other	$39.00 per litre
22060010	Shandy	$26.00 per litre
22060090	Other fermented beverages	$26.00 per litre
22071000	Undenatured ethyl alcohol of an alcoholic strength by volume of 80 per cent or higher	$18.59 per litre
22072000	Ethyl alcohol and other spirits, denatured, of any strength	$1.72 per litre
22082010	Brandy, in bottles of a strength not exceeding 46 per cent volume	$45.50 per litre
22082090	Brandy, other	$45.50 per litre
22083010	Whiskies, in bottles of a strength not exceeding 46 per cent volume	$45.50 per litre
22083090	Whiskies, other	$45.50 per litre
22084010	Rum and tafia in bottles of a strength not exceeding 46 per cent volume	$45.50 per litre
22084090	Rum and tafia, other	$45.50 per litre
22085010	Gin and Geneva, in bottles of a strength not exceeding 46 per cent volume	$45.50 per litre
22085090	Gin and Geneva, other	$45.50 per litre
22086000	Vodka	$52.00 per litre
22087000	Liqueurs and cordials	$52.00 per litre
22089010	Aromatic bitters used as a flavouring agent for food and beverages	$1.43 per litre
22089020	Other aromatic bitters	$18.59 per litre
22089090	Other aromatic bitters, other	$18.59 per litre
21069080	Preparations, other than those based on odoriferous substances	$35.00 per litre
37061000	Cinematographic film, exposed and developed, whether or not incorporating sound track or consisting only of sound track, of a width of 35 mm or more	$3.00 per 100 metres
37069000	Cinematographic film exposed and developed, other	$3.00 per 100 metres

Source: WTO, *Trade Policy Review of Trinidad and Tobago 2005*, Table III.4.

TABLE 7
Import Surcharges, 1999–2005

HS 2002 Heading (HS original heading)	Description of Goods	MFN Tariff Rate	Bound Rate 2004	Rates of Surcharge							Compound Rate 2005
				1999	2000	2001	2002	2003	2004	2005	
02073400 (020731)	Fatty livers of geese or ducks	40	110	98	96	93	91	88	86	40	96
02073500 (020739)	Other meat of ducks	40	110	98	96	93	91	88	86	40	96
02071410 (0207411)	Backs and necks of fowl of the species Gallus domesticus	40	110	98	96	93	91	88	86	40	96
02071420 (0207412)	Wings of fowl of the species Gallus domesticus	40	110	98	96	93	91	88	86	40	96
02071490 (0207419)	Other, of fowl of the species Gallus domesticus	40	110	98	96	93	91	88	86	40	96
02072710 (0207421)	Backs, necks and wings of turkeys	40	100	98	96	93	91	88	86	40	96
02072790 (0207429)	Other, of turkeys	40	100	98	96	93	91	88	86	40	96
02073 (020743)	Meat and edible offal of ducks, geese or guinea fowl	40	100	98	96	93	91	88	86	86	160.4
1701	Cane or beet sugar and chemically pure sucrose, in solid form	40	100	60	60	60	60	60	60	60	124
17019910 (ex1701)	Icing sugar	25	100	75	75	75	75	75	75	75	118.8

Source: WTO, Trade Policy Review of Trinidad and Tobago 2005, Table III.5.

ad valorem equivalents (AVEs) and can also penalise imports of beverages which have lower prices and may compete with domestic production.[10]

Trinidad and Tobago applies import surcharges on a limited number of agricultural products, mainly poultry and sugar, at rates of 40 per cent and 86 per cent (poultry) and 60 per cent and 75 per cent (sugar) (Table 7). The system was introduced in 1990, to provide protection, on a temporary basis, for locally produced goods in the period of transition to complete tariffication of the trade regime. However, the system remained in place after the process was completed. Over the period, however, the list of products subject to surcharges has been trimmed gradually, through both reductions and the phasing-out of rates. Thus most of the surcharges listed in the 1998 Review (mainly on meat and fruit and vegetables) were eliminated by 1999.[11] In early 2004, the only remaining surcharges were on various parts of poultry at 86 per cent and on sugar at 60 per cent.

Through its Uruguay Round and pre-Uruguay Round commitments, Trinidad and Tobago has bound all of its tariffs in the WTO. The average bound tariff is 57.2 per cent while average bound rates are 89.9 per cent for agricultural products (WTO definition) and 50.8 per cent for non-agricultural products (see Table 5). A number of products were bound prior to the Uruguay Round at rates lower than the Uruguay Round bindings, and, in some cases, lower than the currently applied CET rates. Consequently, the MFN schedule includes 44 lines for which MFN rates applied in 2004 were higher than bound rates. These included products such as some live trees and plants, peas, beans, pepper, lime, photographic films, furs, umbrellas, tiles, cubes and similar articles of stone, and some railway construction material. According to authorities this situation can be explained by the fact that the pre-Uruguay Round bindings were not taken into account when the CET was developed.

Trinidad and Tobago only applies CARICOM preferential rules of origin.[12] The country introduced revised rules of origin in 1998, notification of which was given to the WTO in 1999. These have been applied since early 2004. Goods are granted Common Market origin if they have been: (a) wholly produced within CARICOM; or (b) produced within CARICOM wholly or partly from materials imported from third countries, provided a substantial transformation has taken place within CARICOM (Table 8). Substantial transformation may be achieved by change of tariff heading, or may be defined specifically for each tariff heading in Part A of the List in Schedule II of the CARICOM Treaty.

---

[10] Due to the absence of figures to allow the estimation of *ad valorem* equivalents (AVEs) of the specific duties, all calculations of tariff statistics exclude the 27 lines on which specific duties are applied.

[11] The Miscellaneous Taxes (Seventh Schedule) (Amendment) Order, 1997, Legal Notice No. 63 (4 April, 1997).

[12] The country notified the WTO that it maintains no non-preferential rules of origin (WTO, *Trade Policy Review: Trinidad and Tobago 2005*).

TABLE 8
CARICOM Rules of Origin

Product	Rules of Origin
A range of: meat products; fish; vegetables (frozen, preserved or dried); fruits (frozen, preserved or dried) and nuts; products of milling industry; oil seeds; vegetable materials; cocoa beans; sugar; molasses	Wholly produced
A range of: oils; animal products; sugar confectionery; vegetable, fruit and nut preparations; mineral waters; liqueurs and other spirituous beverages; vinegar; wood, wood products and carpentry work; wicker work; ceramic products; articles of cement; articles of plaster; articles of glass; jewellery; gold and silver in semi-manufactured forms; steel products	Produced from regional materials
A range of chemical products included in HS Chapters 28–39	Produced by chemical transformation
A range of plastics products	Non-regional material content must not exceed 10 per cent of the export price of the finished product
Articles of apparel, clothing, accessories and other articles of fur skin (HS 43.03)	Produced from materials not included in HS 43.03 and not being fur skins assembled in plates, crosses or similar forms
Dyed or printed fabrics	Value of extra-regional materials must not exceed 30 per cent of the export price of the finished product
Paper products; a range of products included in HS Chapters 73–96: copper, nickel and aluminium and articles thereof; lead, tin and zinc and articles thereof; other base metals; miscellaneous articles of base metal; tools; machinery and mechanical appliances; boilers; electrical machinery and parts; railway or tramway locomotives and parts thereof; vehicles other than railway and tramway locomotives and parts thereof; aircraft and parts thereof; ships and boats and floating structures; optical, photographic, cinematographic, measuring, checking, medical or surgical instruments and apparatus and parts and accessories; clocks and watches; musical instruments; furniture; arms and ammunition; toys; miscellaneous articles	Value of extra-regional materials must not exceed 50 per cent of the export price of the finished product

Source: WTO, *Trade Policy Review: Trinidad and Tobago 2005*, Table III.1.

(ii) Trinidad and Tobago's trade policy in the context of the CET

Trinidad and Tobago pursues its trade policy initiatives in a manner that recognises that its obligations under both regional and bilateral trade agreements are in fact complementary to those at the multilateral level. Thus as a member of CARICOM, Trinidad and Tobago has applied the regional grouping's Common External Tariff (CET) since 1 January, 1991.[13] Based on the Harmonised Commodity Description and Coding System of 2002, the tariff schedule also incorporates Phase IV of the CET's calendar of reductions, including national exceptions to the CET listed in List A (items in respect of which member states wish to encourage national production) and List C (items for which minimum rates have been agreed, but can be increased up to bound levels by members). The CET rates for industrial products range between 0 and 20 per cent, while rates for agricultural goods range between 0 and 40 per cent.

The products included in List A are subject to a maximum customs duty of 40 per cent while those in List C are generally subject to a minimum rate of 30 per cent, with a few exceptions at 35 and 45 per cent. Trinidad and Tobago's List A comprised 93 products, mainly agricultural products, petroleum products, lavatory sets, and household washing machines and dryers. All tariffs applied to items in List A are lower than or equal to the CET. Products included are granted indefinite suspension of the CET.

In terms of List C, a total of 209 tariff lines are included (automobiles, some electrical appliances, precious metals, beer, wine and spirits) and are subject to tariff rates that exceed maximum CET rates, or to specific duties. Applied tariff rates for List C products are determined by the different CARICOM member countries; common rates are determined by all members, but only for reference purposes.

While the CET represents an important step towards the region's integration into the world economy, there is the criticism that this tariff is more uncommon than common because of the provision for different regimes applicable by groups of member states (CARICOM Secretariat, 2005). As a result there is some evidence of high levels of tariff dispersion and effective protection across the region (Stotsky et al., 2000).

In terms of its other CARICOM commitments, Trinidad and Tobago as a leading member implements the Revised Treaty of Chaguaramas, which covers trade policy, services, consumer protection, competition policy, transport policy and agricultural policy, and forms the legal basis for the establishment of the CARICOM Single Market and Economy (CSME). The CSME, premised on the free movement of goods, services and factors of production, was due to be implemented by participating CARICOM members by 31 December, 2005.

---

[13] Trinidad and Tobago adopted the CET in principle in 1976, but it entered into effect only in 1991.

However, due to the lack of readiness of some of the smaller and lesser developed members, the initiative has not been fully operationalised.

(iii) Bilateral and preferential agreements

Trinidad and Tobago has also increasingly sought expanded market access with third countries through CARICOM. The commonly held view is that this process fosters the gradual integration of small economies into the multilateral system and provides breathing space for the development of small firms within such economies. Consequently, there have been bilateral agreements between CARICOM and countries such as the Dominican Republic, Costa Rica, Venezuela, Colombia and Cuba. The agreements with the Dominican Republic and Costa Rica are Free Trade Agreements with built-in agendas towards the completion of outstanding disciplines. The agreement with Venezuela is currently a one-way preferential agreement, whilst the remaining reciprocal agreements (with Colombia and Cuba) are currently more limited in scope. Trinidad and Tobago considers participation to be a useful step towards the effective and beneficial participation of domestic firms in the multilateral system (TPRTT, 2005).

In addition, the review period covers such preferential trading arrangements as the Cotonou Agreement, CARIBCAN and the Caribbean Basin Initiative (CBI). Under the Cotonou Agreement signed between African, Caribbean and Pacific (ACP) countries and the European Union in 2000, future trading relations have been altered. While presently Trinidad and Tobago's exports are afforded preferential access to the EU market, this arrangement is expected to continue only until the beginning of 2008 when new terms for Trinidad and Tobago's exports will enter into force. In keeping with the provisions of the Cotonou Agreement, such terms are currently being negotiated under the CARIFORUM[14]-European Union EPA negotiations. Opinions on the beneficial effects of an EPA with the EU for Caribbean countries in general have been divided (see Greenaway and Milner, 2006; and Thomas, 2005).

The Caribbean Basin Initiative (CBI) which commenced in 1984 under the Caribbean Basin and Economic Recovery Act (CBERA) and later amended through the Caribbean Basin Trade Partnership Act (CBTPA) provides Trinidad and Tobago with preferential access to the United States. Benefits under the CBTPA are available until 2008. The CARIBCAN programme was introduced in 1986 and covers trade, investment and industrial cooperation between Canada and the Commonwealth Caribbean countries. This programme affords Trinidad and Tobago's exports preferential access to the Canadian market.

(iv) Tariff concessions, suspensions and other modifications

The government of Trinidad and Tobago has established several incentive schemes that provide for duty relief, mainly to imports of inputs, capitals goods,

---

[14] CARIFORUM covers the alliance between CARICOM countries and the Dominican Republic.

machinery and equipment. Tariff concessions are mainly used in export-oriented industries or as investment incentives. For example, Section 56 of the Customs Act is the legal basis for the application of the List of Conditional Duty Exemptions to the CET. Trinidad and Tobago applies this mostly to non-competing inputs and capital goods, which are subject to a CET rate of five per cent but are actually imported duty free or at 2.5 per cent. An example of this process is the Resolution contained in Legal Notice No. 44 of 8 April, 2003, that exempted from the CET,[15] goods in the List of Conditional Duty Exemptions to the CET for the period 1 January, 2002, to 31 December, 2004.[16] These concessions were further extended until 31 December, 2007, through a Resolution dated 10 December, 2004.

By contrast, goods included in the List of Items Ineligible for Duty Exemption to the CET may not be exempted (in whole or in part) where they are imported for use in industry, agriculture, fisheries, forestry and mining. Included in this List are items produced in CARICOM countries in quantities which are considered adequate to justify the application of tariff protection (safeguard clause). It includes a wide range of products, mostly agricultural goods, textiles and clothing products, footwear, toiletries and some electrical appliances. These items may only be eligible for exemption from duty if they are imported 'for other approved purposes' and provided they have been made available as gifts or on a concessionary basis.

Section 8A(1) of the Customs Act empowers the Minister of Finance to grant a partial or total waiver or relief from import duties on specific goods upon request by individuals or organisations. This is done through a Common External Tariff (Suspension) or (Reduction) Order. This power has been exercised on several occasions, mostly with respect to medicines and other chemical products and substances, but sometimes also with respect to agricultural goods, cement and other goods.[17] Conversely, duties can also be increased by Order. For example, the Common External Tariff (Variation of Duty) (No. 13) Order, 2002,

---

[15] Under section 56 of the Customs Act, import duty concessions may be granted through a Resolution, by the House of Representatives, for a specified period, to approved enterprises for approved projects. The concessions may apply to any class of goods as specified in the Resolution for use by any specified person for any specified purpose during a period fixed by the Minister, but not later than the date prescribed in the Resolution as the last day on which the exemption is operative (TTTPR, 2005).

[16] The List of Conditional Duty Exemptions is an appendix to the CET that inventories some 53 different items, defined in detail, for which application of the CET may be waived. A CARICOM member may choose not to use some or all of these exemptions and apply the CET instead. The List does not provide HS headings. There is also a List of Commodities Ineligible for Conditional Duty Exemption, which does list articles by HS heading.

[17] Suspension of the CET and zero tariff rates are generally applied to a list of pharmaceutical products, falling within HS headings 3004.901-909. Rates variations for the period June 2003-June 2004 are contained in the Common External Tariff (Suspension) (No. 2) Order, 2003, and the Common External Tariff (Variation of Duty) (No. 2) Order, 2003.

temporarily increased duties on macaroni and spaghetti to 40 per cent (the CET is 20 per cent), between October 2002 and October 2004. Similarly, tariff levels were increased temporarily from a CET of 15 per cent for Portland cement (HS 2523.291) to 60 per cent, for the period 26 March, 2003, to 31 December, 2004; while the Common External Tariff (Variation of Duty) Order, 2004, increased duties for lead acid batteries to 50 per cent from a CET rate of 20 per cent, between 3 February and 31 December, 2004. Alternatively, the suspension of the CET and the resulting variation of duty may also take the form of a (preferential) tariff quota; this has been the case occasionally for imports of bulk raw sugar.[18]

(v) Other duties, taxes and import controls

Among the other duties and taxes applied on imports are a value-added tax (VAT) for imports from all sources, and a common market rate of duty for certain imports from CARICOM countries only. The latter is used as a replacement for the tariff. The VAT is applied on most goods and services at 15 per cent. With regard to imports, it is levied on the c.i.f. value plus import duties and taxes. In the case of the common market rate of duty, this is levied on certain imports from CARICOM countries and the local production of alcoholic beverages, tobacco and petroleum products. The products subject to the common market rate of duty are the same as those subject to excise tax.

Finally, Trinidad and Tobago maintains a Negative List including goods subject to licensing requirements. The system is applied on an MFN basis with the exception of oils and fats. In their notification to the WTO, the Trinidad and Tobago authorities stated that automatic import licensing is used for statistical purposes. Non-automatic licensing is used to administer import restrictions maintained pursuant to bilateral/regional trade agreements, environmental concerns, national security, health concerns and under the Montreal Protocol.

c. Policy Measures Affecting Exports

Trinidad and Tobago levies no export taxes on goods. However, a number of products require export licences from the Ministry of Industry and Trade. The products concerned are included in the Export Negative List (Table 9). While the granting of export allowances under the Corporation Tax Act No. 14 of 1976, which effectively exempted exporters from corporation taxes, was eliminated in January 2000, other mechanisms to encourage exports are still in place. For example, the Finance Act No. 3 of 1994 makes provision for a deduction of 150

---

[18] The Common External Tariff (Suspension) (No. 6) Order, 2002, The Common External Tariff (Variation of Duty) (No. 13) Order, 2002.

TABLE 9

Exports Requiring a Licence

Description of Goods	Reason for Licence
Coral and other aquatic life found in the country's marine environment or riverine environment:	Protection of local heritage
(a) coral, turtle, turtle-eggs, fauna	
(b) aquarium fish	
(c) shrimp, fish, lobster, crustaceans, molluscs or other aquatic invertebrates (frozen)	
All animal species listed in the Convention on International Trade in Endangered Species of Wild Fauna and Flora (CITES) and endangered species of Trinidad and Tobago	Protection of local heritage
Works of art, artefacts and archaeological findings	Protection of local heritage
Clays, crushed limestone, boulders, sand, gravel, plastering sand, porcellanite, argillite, oil, sand	Protection of local heritage
Planting material, including tissue culture and other plant propagation material of (CITES) listed species	Protection of local heritage
Embryos and artificial insemination material	Protection of local heritage
Agricultural machinery	Subsidised item
Re-export of duty-free capital goods, e.g. mining, construction and other industrial machinery	Subsidised item
Re-export of electro-medical or medical electronic equipment	Subsidised item
Items that are subsidised either directly or indirectly: rice, baker's flour, gasoline, kerosene, liquid petroleum gas	Subsidised item[a]
Explosives, firearms, ammunition and ordnance	National security and foreign policy
All goods consigned to a country in which trade restrictions have been imposed as a matter of national policy	National security and foreign policy
Human organs	Public health
Non-ferrous metal scrap and ores	Domestic supply

Note:

[a] The authorities note that in practice, rice, baker's flour, gasoline, kerosene and liquid petroleum gas do not require a licence since they are no longer subsidised.

Source: WTO, *Trade Policy Review of Trinidad and Tobago 2005*, Table III.10.

per cent of promotional expenses wholly or exclusively incurred for creating or promoting expansion into foreign markets (non-CARICOM) of exports of building industry services, goods and agricultural produce shipped in commercial quantities. Additionally, the Fiscal Incentives Act has provisions on incentives to enclave industries. Finally, the Export-Import Bank of Trinidad and Tobago Limited (EXIMBANK), which is wholly owned by the government and is the only official export credit agency in the country, provides financing and insurance to exporters.

5. CONCLUSION AND OVERALL EVALUATION OF TRINIDAD AND TOBAGO'S TRADE REFORMS

There is little doubt that Trinidad and Tobago has made significant progress in the last decade and a half in transforming its trade regime. The reforms that have led to transformation have been undertaken either as part of the IMF/ World Bank-administered Stabilisation and Structural Adjustment Programmes or unilaterally on the authorities' own volition. Further, the move towards an outward-looking trade regime has been complemented and facilitated by sound macroeconomic and exchange rate policies aimed at fostering international competitiveness.

Most of these reforms, however, can be described as being 'first generation', involving the elimination and/or reduction in the level and range of tariff protection and quantitative restrictions mainly on goods and to a lesser extent on services. As a result, few non-price border restrictions to trade remain. These, as suggested by the *Trade Policy Review*, should be eliminated in order to fully realise the benefits of an outward-oriented trade regime. Examples of measures needed to further liberalise include a narrowing of the gap between applied and bound rates to improve predictability; a reduction in the use of anti-dumping measures and a review of the existing sanitary and phytosanitary (SPS), and Technical Barriers to Trade (TBT) regimes.

However, much of the other reforms which the WTO's *Report* argues the country would benefit from can be classified as 'second generation' involving measures which impact on Trinidad and Tobago's legislative and regulatory framework. These reforms can be regarded as critical to the realisation of Trinidad and Tobago's stated overall trade policy objective of positioning itself as a manufacturing base and a commercial, trans-shipment and financial hub of the western hemisphere. Among the industries singled out for further reforms and implementation of pro-competitive measures are telecommunications, port administration and the maritime transport sector, financial services, and a greater closing of the gap between the country's GATS commitments and actual greater openness of the services sector.

There is presently no comprehensive competition policy legislation in Trinidad and Tobago. While there have been efforts to enhance the regulatory framework and reinforce consumer protection, competition policy legislation is pivotal for the effective regulation of anti-competitive business practices. In its absence certain business practices are prohibited and competition policy issues are currently covered under various pieces of sectoral legislation. Therefore, legislation on competition policy needs to be promulgated in order to make commercial activities more certain and transparent and also improve the efficiency with which commercial activities are undertaken.

Another worrying aspect of Trinidad and Tobago's future economic prospects is the over-reliance on hydrocarbons. In fact, the contribution of the sector to the country's GDP and foreign exchange earnings increased in the 1999–2005 period. Further, a significant part of the manufacturing sector is directly dependent on the energy sector for some of its key inputs. This makes Trinidad and Tobago susceptible to global oil and gas price shocks resulting from price fluctuations that are normally associated with these products; a fate the country experienced (with dire economic consequences) at the onset of the 1980s. Therefore all efforts should be aimed at avoiding or at least minimising the consequences of 'boom' and 'bust'. While the establishment of the Revenue Stabilisation Fund is a commendable effort in this regard, the fact that contributions to the fund are in Trinidad and Tobago dollars rather than in US currency – the currency used in the trading of oil and gas – is open to some criticism.

A further important aspect of Trinidad and Tobago's trade policy is diversification of the economy by facilitating expansion of the non-oil manufacturing sectors through the provision of enabling policy legislation and negotiation of trade agreements with third countries.[19] In this regard, the government has identified some sub-sectors for investment promotion and the formation of strategic alliances (through joint-venture arrangements) with foreign partners to develop capability in these sectors that eventually leads to them being internationally competitive. Among the sub-sectors identified are printing and packaging, food and beverages, metal processing, leisure and marine, and information technology/ electronics. To date, however, there is no detailed research (as far as I am aware) of the viability and sustainability of these industries and the requirements needed to become internationally competitive players in them. This issue is one which the policy-makers should elicit the necessary technical studies as well as public discourse to avoid some of the mistakes made in its first attempt at diversification during the first oil boom.

---

[19] Ministry of Trade and Industry online information. Available at: http://www.tradeind.gov.tt/ news/2003/FTAA%20_Trinbago.pdf

REFERENCES

Annual Economic Survey of Trinidad and Tobago 2005 (Central Bank of Trinidad and Tobago).
Asad, A. and S. Rajapatirana (1993), 'Trade Policy Reform in Latin America and the Caribbean in the 1980s', Policy Research Working Paper Series (World Bank).
CARICOM Secretariat (2005), 'Macroeconomic Policy Coordination and Convergence', in D. Pantin (ed.), *The Caribbean Economy: A Reader* (Ian Randle Publishers, Jamaica, WI).
Finger, J. M., F. Ng and I. Soloaga (1998), 'Trade Policies in the Caribbean Countries: A Look at the Positive Agenda', Paper prepared for discussion at the meetings of the Caribbean Group for Cooperation on Economic Development (Washington, DC, June).
Greenaway, D. and C. R. Milner (2006), 'EU Preferential Trading Arrangements with the Caribbean: A Grim Regional Economic Partnership Agreement?', *Journal of Economic Integration*, **21**, 4, 657–80.
Greenaway, D. and C. Nam (1988), 'Industrialisation and Macroeconomic Performance in Developing Countries under Alternative Trade Strategies', *Kyklos*, **41**, 3, 419–35.
Greenaway, D., C. W. Morgan and P. W. Wright (2002), 'Trade Liberalisation and Growth in Developing Countries', *Journal of Development Economics*, **67**, 1, 229–44.
Harrison, P. (2002), *The Impact of Macroeconomic Policies in Trinidad and Tobago: The Firm under Adjustment* (Institute of Social Studies; Palgrave Macmillan, New York).
National Income of Trinidad and Tobago: 1981–1991 (Central Statistical Office Trinidad and Tobago, 1993).
National Income of Trinidad and Tobago: 1990–1994 (Central Statistical Office Trinidad and Tobago, 1996).
St. Cyr, E. (2007), Interview published in *Sunday Express of Trinidad and Tobago* (25 March).
Stotsky, J., E. Suss and S. Tokarick (2000), 'Trade Liberalization in the Caribbean' (SICE Paper downloaded from http://www.sice.oas.org/geograph/caribbean/stotsky.asp).
Thomas, C. Y. (2005), 'The Inversion of Meaning: Trade Policy and the Caribbean Sugar Industry', in D. Pantin (ed.), *The Caribbean Economy: A Reader* (Ian Randle Publishers, Jamaica, WI).
UNECLAC (1999), 'Review of Caribbean Economic and Social Performance in the 1980s and 1990s' (Sub-regional Headquarters for the Caribbean, Port-of-Spain, Trinidad and Tobago).
World Development Report 1987 (World Bank, Washington, DC).
WTO (1998), *Trade Policy Review of Trinidad and Tobago 1998* (Geneva: WTO).
WTO (2005), *Trade Policy Review of Trinidad and Tobago 2005* (Geneva: WTO).

4

More or Less Ambition in the Doha Round: Winners and Losers from Trade Liberalisation with a Development Perspective

Antoine Bouët, Simon Mevel and David Orden

1. INTRODUCTION

WHAT is at stake in the standoff that has arisen in the Doha Round of trade talks? What impact would an agreement based on greater or lesser levels of ambition have on developing countries, whose economies are relatively dependent on agriculture? Three years after the World Trade Organisation (WTO) talks broke down in Cancún, reform of the heavily protected and subsidised agricultural sectors of the United States, Europe and elsewhere among developed and developing countries remains a major impediment to progress. The December 2005 Hong Kong Ministerial and the negotiations that took place in Geneva until suspended in July 2006 showed little finality to the negotiations.

Trade liberalisation is a potential stimulus for development and the Doha Round was launched with the objective of drawing developing countries more fully into the global trade system. Whether a final Doha Round trade agreement will eventually produce something substantially positive for developing countries remains open to question. Trade liberalisation will act especially positively on development and poverty when developing countries have a comparative advantage in agriculture and are penalised by restricted market access. But developing countries are heterogeneous in terms of their own trade policies, the trade barriers they face, and their net agricultural trade positions.

Very helpful comments have been received from an anonymous referee. The authors also thank seminar participants at the FAO and German Marshall Fund of the United States for their suggestions, while taking full responsibility for any errors in the analysis.

FIGURE 1

Protection Applied and Faced Across Agriculture and Manufacturing

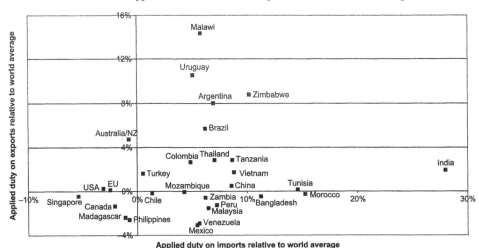

Among the developing countries, some face high tariffs on their exports (for example, Argentina, Brazil, Malawi, Uruguay and Zimbabwe) while others have an above-average access to world markets (Madagascar, Philippines, Venezuela and Malaysia), as shown in Figure 1. Many developing countries impose relatively high tariffs on their imports, while only a few impose tariffs below the world average (Madagascar and Philippines). Both large net food importers and substantial food exporters exist among middle-income countries (MICs) and least developed countries (LDCs). The net trade positions are crucial because trade liberalisation is expected to increase world agricultural prices.

The potential consequences of a Doha agreement have been assessed in a number of recent studies, among them Anderson et al. (2005a and 2005b), Anderson and Martin (2005), Fontagne et al. (2005), Francois et al. (2005) and Bchir et al. (2005). Conclusions diverge, not only on the world real income effect (from 0.04 per cent in Anderson et al., 2005a, to 0.51 per cent in Fontagne et al., 2005), but also on its distribution. This reflects different methodological choices, model parametrisation, and designs of trade reform. The focus of these studies has varied, so they have emphasised different elements of the trade negotiation. For example, while Anderson et al. (2005a) highlight the sensitivity of the potential impact to specific clauses of a trade agreement, Bouët et al. (2005) point out the contrasting benefits and losses for developing countries.

A new feature of the Doha negotiation is that developing countries are actively taking part: the G20 is a largely offensive coalition in terms of liberalisation; the G33 and G90 are more defensive. Their proposals matter but a key issue remains the stance of the United States (US) and the European Union (EU). By late 2005, these two major trading partners had put on the table proposals which have been widely scrutinised and criticised. These two proposals, or modifications to them, remain central to any potential negotiated outcome.

In this article, we take the US and EU proposals as points of reference for what a final outcome of the negotiations might contain. Using the MIRAGE computable general equilibrium model of the global economy we compare different scenarios for the Doha negotiations, taking real numbers from the two proposals, which include substantial detail on agriculture. We compare these two Doha scenarios with full trade liberalisation.[1]

The results for both Doha scenarios demonstrate the high stakes that remain in this negotiation given the positions articulated by the countries involved. An ambitious reform outcome, designed with the most liberalising elements contained in the US and EU proposals, delivers noticeably more benefits than an unambitious outcome, based on the least ambitious components of their negotiating proposals. We scrutinise the development impact of these scenarios and highlight the reasons why trade liberalisation may benefit some developing countries, while having ambiguous effects on others. Eroded preferences and higher world agricultural prices for net food importing countries are critical elements for some developing countries. For this reason, the precise design of the trade reforms is a key issue if the purpose of the Round is development and poverty alleviation.

Section 2 presents the MIRAGE model and analysis of the impact of full trade liberalisation on world real income, world prices and the distribution of gains among countries. Section 3 describes our ambitious and unambitious Doha scenarios. The relative degree of reform of these two scenarios is assessed, first with respect to their impact on world protection, real income and trade volume, and second by the construction of a world Mercantilist Trade Restrictiveness Index. Section 4 focuses on the impact of these two scenarios on developing countries. Section 5 concludes.

2. THE MIRAGE MODEL WITH FULL TRADE LIBERALISATION

a. The MIRAGE Model

The MIRAGE (Modelling International Relationships in Applied General Equilibrium) model is a multi-sector, multi-region CGEM devoted to trade policy

---

[1] The MIRAGE model was developed at the *Centre d'Etudes Prospectives et d'Informations Internationales* (CEPII) in Paris. Full description of the model is available at the CEPII website (www.cepii.fr) and in Bchir et al. (2002).

analysis. The model has a sequential dynamic recursive set-up. Macroeconomic data, in particular social accounting matrices, come from the GTAP6 database (see Dimaranan, 2006).[2] Tariff averages have been re-calculated using the MacMap methodology (see Bouët et al., 2005a and 2005b). Under MacMap, tariff formulae are implemented at the HS6 level before aggregating to the model level and the interplay between bound, MFN applied and preferential duties is fully taken into account.

On the supply side the production function in each sector is a nesting of five primary factors (capital, skilled and unskilled labour, land and natural resources) and intermediate consumption. Factor endowments (except land) are fully employed. Capital supply is modified each year by depreciation and investment. Fixed levels of natural resources and growth rates of labour supply are set exogenously. Land supply is endogenous; utilisation depends on the real rate of remuneration. Installed capital and natural resources are sector-specific. New capital is allocated amongst sectors according to an investment function that depends on the rate of return and the sector stock of capital. Skilled labour is the only factor perfectly mobile. Unskilled labour is imperfectly mobile between agricultural sectors and non-agricultural sectors according to a CET function. Land is also imperfectly mobile among the agricultural sectors.[3]

The demand side is modelled in each region through a representative agent whose propensity to save is constant and whose preferences across sectors are represented by a LES-CES function. Products coming from the 'North' (developed/rich countries) and from the 'South' (developing/poor countries) are assumed to belong to different quality ranges (higher in the North).

The geographic decomposition in our analysis disaggregates the world into 41 countries/zones and 18 sectors in order to capture the heterogeneity among developing countries. Table 1 indicates the geographic regions which include 33 developing countries or aggregated zones. The sector decomposition emphasises the sectors where distortions are high and numerous. Out of the 18 sectors considered, 10 are agricultural and textiles and wearing apparel and leather products are separated from other manufacturing, as shown in Table 2. The last column in Table 2 indicates the agricultural/non-agricultural categorisation that is at the basis of the imperfect mobility of unskilled labour.

In the model equilibrium, perfect competition is assumed in all sectors. With our level of disaggregation, it would have been costly in terms of computational

---

[2] The GTAP6 database provides statistical information for 2001. A pre-experiment was carried out to account for liberalising occurring from 2001 to 2005, including the end of the Uruguay Round, Chinese accession to the WTO, enlargement of the EU, and implementation of the African Growth and Opportunities Act (AGOA) and the EBA initiative.

[3] In MIRAGE, the CET labour substitution elasticity is set at 2. Elasticities of land supply are at the same level as in the LINKAGE model. We thank Dominique Van der Mensbrugghe who kindly provided the land supply parameters.

TABLE 1
Geographic Decomposition

No.	Abbrev.	Region	North/South
1	AUNZ	Australia/New Zealand	North
2	Cana	Canada	North
3	DvdA	Developed Asia	North
4	EU25	European Union	North
5	Mexi	Mexico	North
6	Roec	Rest of OECD	North
7	Turk	Turkey	North
8	USAm	USA	North
9	Arge	Argentina	South
10	Braz	Brazil	South
11	Cari	Caribbean economies	South
12	Chil	Chile	South
13	Chin	China	South
14	Colo	Colombia	South
15	DvgA	Developing Asia	South
16	Indi	India	South
17	Indo	Indonesia	South
18	Mala	Malaysia	South
19	Moro	Morocco	South
20	Peru	Peru	South
21	Phil	Philippines	South
22	SACU	South African Customs Union	South
23	Sing	Singapore	South
24	Thai	Thailand	South
25	Tuni	Tunisia	South
26	Urug	Uruguay	South
27	Vene	Venezuela	South
28	Viet	Vietnam	South
29	Zimb	Zimbabwe	South
30	Bang	Bangladesh	South
31	Mada	Madagascar	South
32	Malw	Malawi	South
33	Moza	Mozambique	South
34	Tanz	Tanzania	South
35	Ugan	Uganda	South
36	Zamb	Zambia	South
37	RAme	Rest of America	South
38	RMen	Rest of Middle East and North Africa	South
39	RSAm	Rest of South America	South
40	RSSA	Rest of Sub-Saharan Africa	South
41	RofW	Rest of the World	South

time to implement imperfect competition in manufacturing, although the MIRAGE model allows this possibility. The model macroeconomic closure is obtained by assuming that the sum of the balance of goods and services for each country/zone is constant and equal to its initial value.

TABLE 2
Sector Decomposition

No.	Abbrev.	Sector	Type of Competition	Agr./ Non-agr.
1	AniP	Animal products and wool	Perfect	Agricultural
2	Meat	Cattle, sheep, goats, horses	Perfect	Agricultural
3	Milk	Raw milk and dairy products	Perfect	Agricultural
4	Plfb	Plant-based fibres	Perfect	Agricultural
5	Rice	Paddy and processed rice	Perfect	Agricultural
6	Sugr	Sugar cane. sugar beet	Perfect	Agricultural
7	VgFr	Vegetables and fruits	Perfect	Agricultural
8	Whet	Wheat	Perfect	Agricultural
9	OtFP	Other food products	Perfect	Agricultural
10	Otag	Other agricultural products	Perfect	Agricultural
11	Mich	Chemical, mineral and metal products	Perfect	Non-agricultural
12	Text	Textiles	Perfect	Non-agricultural
13	Veeq	Vehicles equipment	Perfect	Non-agricultural
14	Weap	Wearing apparel and leather products	Perfect	Non-agricultural
15	Omnf	Other manufactured products	Perfect	Non-agricultural
16	Oprm	Other primary products (including forestry and fishing)	Perfect	Non-agricultural
17	OtSr	Other services	Perfect	Non-agricultural
18	TrT	Transportation and trade	Perfect	Non-agricultural

b. The Potential Impact of Full Trade Liberalisation

To evaluate the effects of full trade liberalisation, reform is implemented over five years from 2006 for developed countries and over 10 years for developing countries. Results are assessed by comparing the simulation outcomes for 2019 to a baseline without any trade reform. Technology is assumed constant in these comparisons; trade reform does not induce productivity gains as assumed in some models.

With full liberalisation, world protection, which initially averages 5.4 per cent across agriculture and manufacturing as measured by a weighted aggregate statistic, is eliminated. Full trade liberalisation implies an increase of world trade volume by 12 per cent and world real income by $158 billion (in constant 2001 dollar value; a gain of +0.5 per cent of expected 2019 world real income in the baseline).

Table 3 indicates the distribution of this income gain among the OECD, MICs and LDCs. Full liberalisation is slightly progressive based on a comparison of initial income levels and income gains between developed and developing countries. For developing countries as a whole, the share of welfare gains (21.2 per cent) is greater than their share of initial world income (18.5 per cent). But the aggregate gain is small (and regressive) for the LDCs – only 0.1 per cent of the

TABLE 3
Impact of Full Trade Liberalisation on World Real Income

	OECD	MIC	LDC
Real income gain ($ bn)	124.2	33.4	0.1
Share in world real income gain	78.7%	21.2%	0.1%
Share in initial world real income	80.6%	18.5%	0.9%
Real income gain (in %)	0.49%	0.58%	0.05%

Source: Authors' calculations.

global income gains accrue to the LDCs compared with their initial share of world income of 0.9 per cent.

The gain in real income in our simulation is smaller than the gain of $287 billion estimated by 2015 using the LINKAGE model by Anderson et al. (2005a and 2005b).[4] To assess the sources of this difference, three sensitivity analyses were undertaken:

- The MIRAGE model utilises GTAP Armington elasticities. Van der Mensbrugghe (2006) calculates that they are on average 35 per cent lower than those utilised in the LINKAGE model, while Harrison et al. (1997) utilises even higher elasticities. If the GTAP Armington trade elasticities are multiplied by 1.5, the world real income gain is $212 billion in 2015 (a gain of +0.71 per cent from the baseline) and $244 billion in 2019 (+0.72 per cent) in our full liberalisation scenario.
- With perfect mobility of unskilled labour across sectors, the world real income gain is only slightly changed to $136 billion in 2015 (+0.45 per cent) and $160 billion in 2019 (+0.51 per cent).
- The LINKAGE model incorporates GDP growth expectations from the World Development Indicators. Our simulations are not scaled up to match these GDP growth projections. Doing so amplifies the value of world real income in the baseline. The world real income gain is $178 billion in 2015 (+0.45 per cent) and $225 billion in 2019 (+0.52 per cent).

The difference in real income gains from full liberalisation between our estimate of $158 billion in 2019 and the assessments carried out by Anderson et al. (2005a and 2005b) comes mainly from the adoption of low trade elasticities. Including GDP growth expectations in the baseline also increases the size of world real income and consequently the size of the gain expressed in dollar value.

---

[4] In 2015, the gain in world real income is $135 billion, +0.45 per cent as compared to the baseline, in our simulation.

FIGURE 2

Impact of Full Liberalisation on Agricultural World Prices

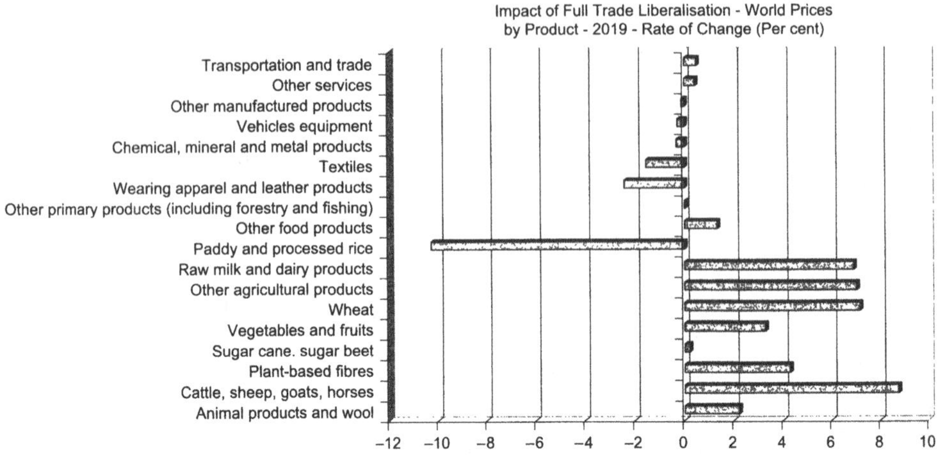

Source: Authors' calculations.

In our simulation, full trade liberalisation implies an expected significant increase in agricultural world prices. Price effects are largest for meat (cattle, sheep, goats, horses), wheat, raw milk and dairy products, and other agricultural products, as shown in Figure 2. The indicative average price changes shown in this figure have to be somewhat carefully interpreted. In the MIRAGE model there is not a single world price for a commodity but separate export prices for each product, for each exporting country and for each destination. The results shown in Figure 2 are weighted average of numerous price evolutions. When the dispersion of a price distribution is high, an average does not synthesise consistently the separate impacts.[5] This is especially the case for rice. Initially, rice is subject to highly dispersed tariffs: 0 per cent in Australia/New Zealand, Canada, Malaysia, SACU, Singapore and Madagascar, but 117 per cent in the EU, 133 per cent in Morocco and 538 per cent in Developed Asia, on average. In Figure 2, the average world price of rice decreases with full trade liberalisation. Because of the high dispersion of protectionism of this commodity in the world, with full liberalisation export prices of rice exhibit large individual increases in countries exporting to previously highly-protected markets and decreases in traditionally

---

[5] This point is confirmed by calculating the average price changes under alternative methods (Laspeyres or Fisher index instead of Paasche index) or with different weights (consumption of the importing country). The alternative measures give contrasting pictures of the evolution of world prices, sometimes with increases in the average world price of rice. Calculation of dispersion indicators of the evolution of world prices by products and exporting countries shows that dispersion is especially high in this sector.

protectionist countries for which reductions in domestic prices are linked with a significant cut in export prices. Country-specific results are not shown, but the average prices of rice exports from Thailand and the US, for example, are raised by 30 per cent, and from Mexico by 20 per cent, Malawi by 15 per cent, Malaysia by 12 per cent and Australia/New Zealand by 10 per cent. Conversely, average export prices decrease by −41 per cent for Developed Asia, which is initially a major rice exporter after Thailand, and by −12 per cent for Developing Asia. Similar dispersed results underlie the small increase of the world average sugar price shown in Figure 2.

Table 4 highlights the diverse country impacts of full trade liberalisation, presenting the total gains, the allocation efficiency gains and the terms of trade gains. The two last columns do not necessarily add up exactly to the real income gain because they are not the only sources of welfare variations. Real income variations also come from changes in land utilisation, from variation in the stock of capital, elimination of tariff-quota rents and other sources.[6] But in most cases the allocation and terms of trade gains are the two main sources of changes to real incomes.

Allocation efficiency gains are usually positive; terms of trade effects can be positive or negative. This explains why some countries/zones may lose from full trade liberalisation (Bangladesh, China, Madagascar, Mexico, Morocco, Mozambique, Peru, Philippines, Venezuela, Zambia and the zone Rest of the World). Others benefit from large increases in real income (Malawi, Malaysia, Turkey, Thailand and Rest of America). Allocation efficiency gains are largest when initial protection is high (India and Morocco), initial protection has a high dispersion across sectors (Rest of OECD and Developed Asia), or in the case of initially very open economies (Malaysia) because the allocation-efficiency effect is amplified when initial imports are relatively large for a given decrease in tariff. Taken overall, the size of the benefits is greater than the losses.

Terms of trade effects are positive for countries gaining access to previously protected markets (for example, Australia/New Zealand for animal products, milk and dairy products, and other food products sectors toward Rest of OECD, Developed Asia, the EU, Canada and Turkey; Malawi in the other agricultural products sector, which account for 65 per cent of its initial exports; Malaysia in rice toward Developed Asia and wheat toward India). On the contrary, full trade liberalisation can imply a deterioration of terms of trade either in the case of erosion of preferential accesses to certain export markets, which implies more competition and reduced export prices, or in the case of net food importing countries facing rising world agricultural prices. Bangladesh and Tunisia are

---

[6] The welfare gains from increased income from reform feeding into augmented savings and capital stock differs from the standard Haberger triangles but they would not have been realised without trade reform.

TABLE 4

Impact of Full Trade Liberalisation on Countries' Real Income

Region		Real Income (in per cent)	Allocation Efficiency Gains (in per cent)	Terms of Trade Gains (in per cent)
High-income countries	Australia/New Zealand	1.5	0.1	1.2
	Canada	0.1	0.3	0.0
	Developed Asia	1.1	1.4	0.1
	European Union	0.5	0.3	0.1
	Mexico	-0.2	0.7	-0.6
	Rest of OECD	3.0	8.4	-0.7
	Turkey	5.2	1.0	2.2
	USA	0.1	0.0	0.1
Middle-income countries	Argentina	1.2	0.2	0.5
	Brazil	0.8	0.3	0.3
	Caribbean economies	0.7	0.6	-0.1
	Chile	0.7	0.2	0.0
	China	-0.1	1.0	-0.8
	Colombia	0.2	0.2	-0.1
	Developing Asia	0.8	0.8	0.1
	India	0.3	1.9	-1.4
	Indonesia	1.5	0.2	0.3
	Malaysia	8.0	9.3	1.7
	Morocco	-0.1	2.5	-3.2

Peru	-0.3	0.3	-0.6
Philippines	-0.1	0.4	-1.1
Rest of America	4.8	7.7	-0.3
Rest of Middle East and North Africa	0.1	0.4	-0.3
Rest of South America	3.1	0.7	1.4
Rest of the World	-0.1	0.4	-0.5
South African Customs Union	1.1	0.6	0.3
Singapore	2.3	0.0	2.0
Thailand	4.9	2.0	0.8
Tunisia	1.6	3.6	-3.0
Uruguay	1.8	0.4	0.3
Venezuela	-0.5	0.2	-0.5
Vietnam	3.3	2.7	-1.2
Zimbabwe	3.1	1.3	1.6
Low-income countries			
Bangladesh	-0.5	1.3	-1.7
Madagascar	-0.3	0.0	-0.4
Malawi	11.2	1.4	7.3
Mozambique	-0.2	0.4	-0.7
Rest of Sub-Saharan Africa	0.1	1.4	-1.3
Tanzania	0.7	0.6	-0.3
Uganda	0.5	0.1	0.3
Zambia	-0.6	0.6	-1.0

Source: Authors' calculations.

affected by a substantial deterioration of terms of trade both owing to erosion of preferences (Europe is by far their primary export destination) and higher agricultural prices.[7] Erosion of preferences also hurts Madagascar, Mexico, Morocco, Mozambique, Tanzania, Zambia, Rest of OECD, Rest of MENA and Rest of Sub-Saharan Africa. As net food importing countries, China, Philippines and Venezuela are hurt by raising world agricultural prices.

The case of China is interesting as initially China is a net exporter of vehicle equipment, textile and apparel and chemical products while it is a net importer of wheat, rice and plant-based fibres. Full trade liberalisation entails a large increase of its exports, but also of its imports as its initial rate of protection is much higher than the average duty faced on its exports. China's domestic activity is significantly stimulated (by about five per cent) but its terms of trade deteriorate as agricultural world prices increase. In the textile and apparel sectors, Chinese export prices decrease due to competitive effects: trade liberalisation has a larger effect on production and exports of textiles and apparel of Malaysia, Vietnam, India, Philippines and other Developing Asia countries than on Chinese production. Overall, full trade liberalisation entails a significant reorganisation of the world production and trade of textiles and apparel. China increases its market share but is not by far the first beneficiary. Textile and apparel sectors in OECD countries and LDCs (except Bangladesh) are negatively affected. In terms of total welfare for China, with full liberalisation terms of trade deterioration is compensated by allocative efficiency gains and welfare gains are close to zero.

The deterioration in terms of trade implied by full liberalisation in the cases of India, Peru and Vietnam (initially net food exporters) and improvement in the case of Singapore (net food importer) are less intuitive. These cases demonstrate that aggregated indicators can be misleading. The initial net food balance of a country is not an unambiguous indicator of how national terms of trade will be affected by trade liberalisation. Distortions are unevenly distributed across products and import and export structure of trading partners are very different. While Peru, for example, is globally a net food exporter, its exports are highly concentrated in chemical, mineral and metal products (37 per cent of total exports in 2005) and other food products (16 per cent). The latter commodity experiences one of the smallest increases in world prices amongst the agro-food products. Furthermore, the price of the former is negatively affected by full trade liberalisation. As a result, Peru is affected by a deterioration of its terms of trade after full liberalisation.

A few countries also benefit especially from liberalisation-related resource utilisation gains. For example, agricultural activity increases in Argentina, Malawi and Australia/New Zealand, raising the real remuneration of land, especially as

---

[7] The methodology adopted here implicitly supposes that preferences are fully utilised. This may underestimate the importance of trade barriers in some cases, for example, in the case of Bangladesh's exports of apparel to the European Union on which rules of origin are known to be strict.

it is not a very mobile primary factor. This accordingly increases land utilisation and amplifies national real income gains from trade reform.

3. AMBITIOUS VERSUS UNAMBITIOUS DOHA REFORM SCENARIOS

In the Doha Round negotiations, criticism has been directed at developed countries for protecting and subsidising agriculture, which stifles trade opportunities. Yet, the US and EU follow somewhat different regimes. The US has relatively low tariffs, but its domestic agricultural support was increased in the most recent (2002) farm bill. The US provides relatively less preferential access than does the EU for selected developing-country trade partners. The EU, in contrast, has higher agricultural (but similarly low industrial) tariffs and has recently realigned its relatively high levels of agricultural support toward policy instruments that are less trade distorting than in the past. In these US–EU policy differences lie the seeds of different approaches to the trade negotiations.

a. Similarities and Differences in the US and EU Proposals of 2005

The US and EU proposals of late 2005 have some broad commonalities, such as progressive tariff and domestic support cuts and the elimination of export subsidies. But the specifics of the proposals diverge on matters such as rates of reduction of tariffs and domestic agricultural support and the number of agricultural sensitive or special products (for developed and developing countries, respectively) that will be subject to lesser disciplines. In terms of an ambitious agenda for agricultural trade liberalisation, strong points of the US proposal include sharper reductions in bound tariff rates and a lower cap on maximum allowable tariffs, few sensitive or special products, and moderately tough bindings on domestic support that encourage decoupling of subsidies from production. Strong points of the EU proposal in terms of trade liberalisation lie in the call for free access of LDCs to OECD markets, a specific initiative for cotton to help West Africa, and a push for lower industrial tariffs worldwide.

b. What Difference Could a Doha Outcome Make?

What difference could a Doha Round outcome make to global trade and welfare and to developing countries in particular? To examine this question, we define a relatively ambitious cooperative reform scenario with strong trade liberalisation components from the US and EU proposals using numbers on the negotiating table at the December 2005 Hong Kong ministerial meeting, and contrast this with a less ambitious outcome drawn from the lower-end elements (see Box 1).

BOX 1
Overview of Two Scenarios

AMBITIOUS SCENARIO

Tariffs:

- US tariff formula for agriculture
- Tariff caps in agriculture (developed countries, 100 per cent; developing countries, 150 per cent)
- US sensitive/special products clause (one per cent)
- Swiss formula cuts for manufacturing tariffs (developed-country coefficient, eight per cent; MIC coefficient, 20 per cent; LDC coefficient, 30 per cent)
- EU proposal of free OECD access for LDCs

Domestic support levels cut by 20 per cent
Export subsidies eliminated

UNAMBITIOUS SCENARIO

Tariffs:

- EU tariff formula for agriculture
- No agricultural tariff caps
- EU-sensitive/special products clause (eight per cent)
- Swiss formula cuts for manufacturing tariffs (developed-country coefficient, 10 per cent; MIC coefficient, 30 per cent)
- LDCs do not reduce their import duties
- Additional free OECD access for LDCs, but exceptions for Japan and South Korea (rice) and the US (sugar, textiles and apparel)

Domestic support levels unchanged
Export subsidies are eliminated

On market access, our ambitious proposal includes most elements of the US formula.[8] It adds the EU proposal for free access by LDCs to OECD markets, imposes tariff caps in agriculture and defines an exception regime for sensitive/

---

[8] The US proposal prior to the December 2005 Hong Kong meeting called for cuts of 85–90 per cent in agricultural tariffs above 60 per cent for developed countries and lesser cuts in three bands of lower initial tariffs. The EU called for less ambitious cuts of 60 per cent in agricultural tariffs above 90 per cent for developed countries and similarly less ambitious cuts for lower initial tariff bands. The US proposal involves a quadratic transformation of original tariffs under which final tariffs go down as original tariffs go up over a substantial range. The ambitious scenario keeps this apparent 'inconsistency'. The tariff-cutting formula for developing countries is applied to LDCs as well as MICs, a point not addressed explicitly in the US proposal.

TABLE 5
Global Results of Alternative Liberalisation Scenarios

	World Protection (Per cent)	Real Income Gain (Per cent)	World Trade (Per cent)
Full trade liberalisation	−5.4	$158.0 bn	12.0
Ambitious scenario	−1.9	$76.7 bn	2.8
	(35)	(49)	(23)
Unambitious scenario	−1.2	$38.3 bn	1.6
	(22)	(24)	(13)

Source: MacMaps-HS6 and authors' calculations.

special products of only one per cent of agricultural tariff lines per country.[9] Applied trade-distorting domestic agricultural support is cut by 20 per cent and relatively strong manufacturing tariff reductions are imposed on developed and developing countries (including LDCs) under a three-tier Swiss formula.

In contrast to the ambitious scenario, our unambitious scenario adopts the EU formula for less deep tiered tariff cuts for agriculture, does not impose any cap on agricultural tariffs, exempts LDCs from agricultural tariff cuts, and adds fewer liberalising elements on sensitive/special products (exceptions for eight per cent of tariff lines), the tariff-reduction Swiss formula for industry (higher tariff targets for developed countries and MICs and no cuts by LDCs) and free OECD access for LDCs (some exceptions are retained). No cuts are assumed in applied domestic agricultural support of developed countries.

c. *Global Results for the Ambitious versus Unambitious Doha Scenarios*

As shown in Table 5, the unambitious scenario leads to global real income gains of only $38.3 billion, just 24 per cent of the gain from full liberalisation. World protection measured by the weighted aggregate statistic declines by 1.2 per cent. This is 22 per cent of the decline (to zero protection) with full liberalisation. World trade expands 1.6 per cent, which is only 13 per cent of the expansion induced by full trade liberalisation.

A substantially greater movement is observed under the ambitious scenario. Global welfare increases by $76.7 billion, 49 per cent of the gain from full liberalisation. World protection falls by 1.9 per cent (35 per cent of the effect of

---

[9] Sensitive/Special Products are here defined as the lines supporting the highest bound tariffs, expressed in *ad valorem* terms. Our later research (Bouët et al., 2006) utilises a more sophisticated definition on the basis of a political economy model, like Jean et al. (2005).

78   ANTOINE BOUËT, SIMON MEVEL AND DAVID ORDEN

full liberalisation). World trade is increased by 2.8 per cent, which is 23 per cent of the expansion with free trade.

For both the trade expansion and gains of real income, the unambitious scenario yields outcomes about half as large as the ambitious scenario (13 per cent/ 23 per cent for trade expansion and 24 per cent/49 per cent for real income compared with the free trade outcomes, respectively). These ratios provide an estimate of what is *still* at stake in a conclusion to the Doha negotiations. A key factor differentiating the ambitious from unambitious scenario is the degree of increased market access in agriculture. Under the ambitious scenario, agricultural protection decreases by 8.7 per cent from an initial global average of 17.8 per cent. Under the unambitious scenario, agricultural protection falls by only three per cent.

d. An Evaluation by an MTRI

Another way of assessing the degree of ambition of these two scenarios is the construction of a Mercantilist Trade Restrictiveness Index (MTRI): it is a uniform tariff applied to all imports of a country that provides the same level of import volumes as the existing distortions (see Anderson and Neary, 1999). The focus on import volumes is consistent with the character of trade negotiations under the WTO. To determine the MTRI, we substitute into a static version of the MIRAGE model a uniform tariff on all imports of all countries from all partners in the world for existing tariffs, domestic support and export subsidies at the model level of aggregation. We then search for the level of this uniform tariff that generates the same world imported volume as (i) the existing distortions in 2005, (ii) the unambitious scenario and (iii) the ambitious scenario.

Table 6 gives the results of this calculation. The 2005 situation is equivalent in terms of world imports to a uniform four per cent tariff. This is smaller than the weighted average tariff, but it also includes the impact of export subsidies on trade. The initial MTRI might also mean that the MacMap method of aggregation overestimates the distortive impact of high tariffs in agriculture.

TABLE 6
MTRI from Alternative Liberalisation Scenarios

	MTRI (Per cent)
Current situation	4.00
Unambitious scenario	3.20
	(−20)
Ambitious scenario	2.60
	(−35)

Source: Authors' calculations.

Under the unambitious scenario the MTRI is 3.2 per cent, which is a 20 per cent decline in world protection. Under the ambitious scenario the MTRI is 2.6 per cent; this represents a 35 per cent drop in protection. The MTRI revises downwards the degree of initial distortion but the relative MTRI results for the two Doha scenarios are similar to the earlier estimates of reductions in average world protection (22 per cent reduction under the unambitious scenario and 35 per cent under the ambitious scenario). This consistent distortion aggregation measure somewhat reduces the relative stakes in the outcome of the negotiations, because the new range is only 20 per cent/35 per cent instead of the 24 per cent/ 49 per cent previously calculated in terms of world real income. A possible explanation is that a tariff increase on a low tariff good has a large adverse impact on market access and trade because a low-tariff good implies, other things being equal, high trade value.[10] This result also verifies recent literature on the MTRI (see Anderson and Neary, 2004) which demonstrates that higher tariff variance means higher welfare gains, but smaller trade gains.

4. POTENTIAL IMPACT OF A DOHA AGREEMENT ON DEVELOPING COUNTRIES

The ambitious and unambitious scenarios are quite different in terms of liberalisation effects at the world level. It remains to describe whether they imply contrasting fortunes for developing countries.

a. Impact on Market Access

The impact of the two scenarios on agricultural market access as measured by applied tariff levels of selected countries is illustrated in Figure 3. The ambitious scenario implies a much larger liberalisation in rich countries where protection is initially high and unevenly distributed. The average agricultural protection is reduced more by the ambitious compared with the unambitious scenario in the EU, Developed Asia and the Rest of OECD. This confirms that the imposition of a cap on agricultural tariffs and limited exemptions from tariff liberalisation under sensitive/special product clauses have large consequences on market access, as discussed by Anderson and Martin (2005).

The binding overhang phenomenon is so large in developing countries that even the ambitious scenario has a mitigated impact in agricultural protection except in India and Morocco, as also discussed by Jean et al. (2005). Under the unambitious scenario protection in LDCs is unchanged; and likewise even the ambitious scenario implies little applied tariff reduction by LDCs.

---

[10] Thanks to the anonymous referee who suggested this explanation.

Agricultural protection before and after a potential Doha agreement (Applied duties)

□ Initial protection (2005)   ■ After ambitious scenario   □ After unambitious scenario

Source: MacMaps-HS6 and authors' calculations.

b. Impact on Real Incomes

The heterogeneity among developing countries is illustrated by divergence in the real-income effects of the two Doha scenarios (see Table 7). The degree of ambition makes quite a difference for developing countries. Under the unambitious scenario, Zambia, Madagascar, Venezuela, Mexico, the Rest of Sub-Saharan Africa and the Rest of the World are losers, while under the ambitious scenario only Venezuela and Zambia lose from global trade reform. Furthermore, under the ambitious scenario benefits are larger for all developing countries, except Zambia.

In terms of individual MICs that might benefit from trade liberalisation, the unambitious scenario delivers very little real income gain for two reasons. First, these countries gain little from improved terms of trade despite the reduced protection among wealthy countries. Second, they gain little from allocation efficiency largely because they make so few changes to their own policies. The same results occur for the LDCs that might gain from trade liberalisation – terms of trade gains and allocation efficiency gains are very small under the unambitious scenario. Only Malawi and Malaysia obtain large benefits under both scenarios, the former from large terms of trade gains and the latter because of its high trade/GDP ratio.

Under the ambitious scenario, developing countries gain more from trade reform. Among the MICs, allocation efficiency gains are larger under the ambitious scenario than under the unambitious scenario, but they remain less than in the case of full liberalisation. In case of positive terms of trade effects, gains are larger under the ambitious scenario owing to increased market access.

TABLE 7

Effects of Alternative Liberalising Scenarios on Real Income

Region		Ambitious Scenario			Unambitious Scenario		
		Real Income (in per cent)	Allocation Efficiency Gains (in per cent)	Terms of Trade Gains (in per cent)	Real Income (in per cent)	Allocation Efficiency Gains (in per cent)	Terms of Trade Gains (in per cent)
High-income countries	Australia/New Zealand	0.7	0.1	0.5	0.4	0.1	0.2
	Canada	0.1	0.1	0.0	0.0	0.0	0.0
	Developed Asia	0.3	0.6	-0.1	0.1	0.1	0.0
	European Union	0.2	0.2	0.0	0.1	0.0	0.0
	Mexico	0.1	0.3	-0.2	0.0	0.2	-0.1
	Rest of OECD	2.9	7.0	-0.6	2.4	6.3	-0.4
	Turkey	4.0	0.3	1.8	3.8	0.2	1.8
	USA	0.0	0.0	0.0	0.0	0.0	0.0
Middle-income countries	Argentina	0.3	0.1	0.1	0.2	0.0	0.1
	Brazil	0.3	0.1	0.1	0.1	0.1	0.0
	Caribbean economies	0.4	0.2	0.2	0.2	0.1	0.1
	Chile	0.2	0.0	0.1	0.1	0.0	0.0
	China	0.4	0.0	0.2	0.4	0.0	0.2
	Colombia	0.2	0.1	0.1	0.0	0.0	0.0
	Developing Asia	0.5	0.3	0.1	0.3	0.1	0.1
	India	0.4	0.8	-0.5	0.3	0.7	-0.4
	Indonesia	0.5	0.1	0.1	0.5	0.0	0.2
	Malaysia	3.4	4.7	-0.6	2.9	3.9	-0.6
	Morocco	0.5	1.5	-1.2	0.4	1.1	-0.9
	Peru	0.0	0.0	0.0	0.1	0.0	0.0
	Philippines	0.1	0.1	-0.1	0.1	0.0	0.0
	Rest of America	0.8	0.1	0.9	0.2	0.0	0.1
	Rest of Middle East and North Africa	0.1	0.2	-0.1	0.0	0.1	-0.1
	Rest of South America	0.9	0.2	0.3	0.0	0.1	-0.2

TABLE 7 Continued

Region	Ambitious Scenario			Unambitious Scenario		
	Real Income (in per cent)	Allocation Efficiency Gains (in per cent)	Terms of Trade Gains (in per cent)	Real Income (in per cent)	Allocation Efficiency Gains (in per cent)	Terms of Trade Gains (in per cent)
Rest of the World	0.0	0.1	0.0	-0.1	0.0	-0.1
South African Customs Union	0.4	0.3	0.1	0.2	0.2	0.0
Singapore	0.3	0.0	0.3	0.1	0.0	0.1
Thailand	1.4	1.0	-0.1	0.7	0.8	-0.3
Tunisia	1.8	1.8	-0.8	0.8	1.0	-0.6
Uruguay	0.7	0.1	0.2	0.2	0.1	0.0
Venezuela	-0.3	0.1	-0.3	-0.3	0.0	-0.2
Vietnam	0.7	0.0	0.4	0.5	0.0	0.3
Zimbabwe	0.7	0.6	0.1	0.3	0.4	-0.1
Low-income countries						
Bangladesh	2.3	0.9	1.0	0.3	0.0	0.2
Madagascar	2.6	0.0	2.0	-0.1	0.0	-0.1
Malawi	5.1	0.8	3.3	5.1	0.0	3.3
Mozambique	1.4	0.1	0.9	0.1	0.0	0.0
Rest of Sub-Saharan Africa	1.2	0.8	0.2	0.0	0.3	-0.3
Tanzania	0.2	0.1	0.0	0.2	0.0	0.1
Uganda	0.2	0.0	0.2	0.2	0.0	0.2
Zambia	-0.2	0.1	-0.1	-0.1	0.0	0.1

Source: Authors' calculations.

In the case of LDCs a few cases are remarkable. Bangladesh is a full beneficiary of the ambitious scenario. Its preferences from the EU are eroded but the ambitious scenario gives it free access to the US in the textile and apparel markets. Because of this full coverage of free access by LDCs to OECD markets, Bangladesh's exports of textiles to the US increase by 58 per cent in the ambitious scenario instead of 32 per cent in the unambitious scenario and apparel by 46 per cent instead of 13 per cent.[11] Under the ambitious scenario prices of textile and apparel exports from Bangladesh to the EU and US markets are from 9–12 per cent higher than under full trade liberalisation, as it benefits from preferential LDC access. It also gains from allocative efficiency under the ambitious scenario, so this trade reform is unambiguously more beneficial than the unambitious outcome. The same mechanisms, with different size, play out for Madagascar and Rest of Sub-Saharan Africa.

On the contrary full trade liberalisation implies larger increases in agricultural world prices and complete erosion of preferences compared with the ambitious Doha scenario. As a result, terms of trade losses implied by full liberalisation (shown in Table 4) are substantial among LDCs for Bangladesh (–1.7 per cent) and the Rest of Sub-Saharan Africa (–1.3 per cent) and decline also for Mozambique (–0.7 per cent) and Madagascar (–0.4 per cent).

c. Impact on Productive Factors

On poverty also the degree of ambition of the Doha trade reform might make a difference. Table 8 compares the effects on remuneration of productive factors under the two scenarios. To the extent that the unskilled real wage is indicative of poverty effects, the ambitious scenario delivers more poverty reduction. Unskilled workers are better off under the ambitious outcome compared to the unambitious outcome in all countries/zones except Malaysia, Venezuela and Zambia. The differences in gains to unskilled real wages are particularly noticeable for Bangladesh, Madagascar, Mozambique, Rest of Sub-Saharan Africa, Rest of America, Rest of South America, Thailand and Uruguay. There are also larger gains to agricultural real wages under the ambitious scenario in all but a few countries.

A comparison with real wage results obtained in the two Doha scenarios to full trade liberalisation is also instructive.[12] Unskilled labour benefits much more from full liberalisation than from partial liberalisation in Argentina, Brazil, Chile, Indonesia, SACU, Thailand, Zimbabwe, Vietnam, Uruguay and Malawi. These benefits come mainly from large gains for agricultural unskilled labour.

---

[11] These results highlight the negative consequence for LDCs of the exclusion of three per cent of tariff lines from the free-access agreement reached in Hong Kong. See Bouët et al. (2005) for quantitative analysis of this provision in isolation.
[12] The free trade results are not shown in Table 8 but are available from the authors on request.

TABLE 8
Effects of Alternative Liberalising Scenarios on Remunerations

Region		Unskilled Real Wages	Unskilled Real Wages in Agriculture	Unskilled Real Wages in Non-agricultural Sectors	Real Return to Capital	Real Return to Land	Real Return to Natural Resources	Skilled Real Wages
		Ambitious scenario						
High-income countries	Australia/New Zealand	1.3	5.0	1.0	0.2	2.0	-2.0	0.8
	Canada	0.0	1.2	0.0	0.2	-4.7	0.5	0.0
	Developed Asia	0.3	-7.2	0.4	0.5	-16.9	1.3	0.6
	European Union	0.2	-1.0	0.3	-0.3	-10.4	1.7	0.5
	Mexico	-0.1	-1.0	0.0	0.0	-2.8	0.1	0.3
	Rest of OECD	2.8	-4.2	2.9	1.7	-15.3	5.3	3.5
	Turkey	4.0	2.1	4.4	3.4	-3.1	-6.2	7.3
	USA	0.0	1.7	0.0	0.1	-1.8	0.2	-0.1
Middle-income countries	Argentina	0.7	2.5	0.6	0.2	2.2	-2.5	0.6
	Brazil	0.4	2.2	0.3	0.2	2.4	-1.9	0.3
	Caribbean economies	1.0	3.3	0.7	0.3	3.4	-3.7	0.2
	Chile	0.5	1.4	0.3	-0.1	1.2	-0.9	0.3
	China	0.7	1.2	0.5	-0.3	1.4	-1.3	0.7
	Colombia	0.5	2.9	0.2	-0.4	3.3	-2.1	-0.2
	Developing Asia	0.6	0.3	0.7	0.1	0.0	-0.3	0.7
	India	0.5	0.5	0.5	-1.3	0.6	-11.6	1.7

Indonesia	0.6	0.7	0.6	-0.1	0.4	-0.2	0.4
Malaysia	-1.5	-2.1	-1.5	-4.5	-4.0	-16.3	-1.0
Morocco	0.7	0.7	0.7	-0.3	0.5	-5.4	0.5
Peru	0.1	0.4	0.0	0.0	0.1	-0.7	-0.1
Philippines	0.5	0.5	0.5	-0.1	0.2	-0.5	0.2
Rest of America	2.6	7.6	1.4	0.0	8.1	-5.2	0.2
Rest of Middle East and North Africa	0.0	0.1	-0.1	0.0	0.2	1.3	-0.2
Rest of South America	1.6	4.1	1.0	-0.8	3.8	-6.4	0.2
Rest of the World	0.2	0.5	0.1	0.0	0.8	-0.3	-0.1
South African Customs Union	0.3	1.5	0.2	0.2	1.4	2.9	0.2
Singapore	0.4	7.2	0.3	0.2	-1.0	-0.3	0.2
Thailand	1.5	2.5	1.2	-0.3	2.5	-5.8	1.1
Tunisia	1.2	-0.5	1.6	1.5	-3.0	-1.7	2.1
Uruguay	1.3	2.6	1.0	0.0	1.7	-3.0	1.1
Venezuela	-0.1	0.5	-0.2	-0.3	0.9	-1.8	-0.3
Vietnam	1.5	2.1	1.3	0.0	2.4	1.0	1.3
Zimbabwe	0.8	1.6	0.5	0.4	1.2	0.1	0.4
Low-income countries — Bangladesh	1.9	6.8	0.9	1.1	11.3	-3.3	0.7
Madagascar	7.3	12.4	2.4	-4.3	7.4	-4.7	-1.4
Malawi	4.6	3.8	5.1	6.2	-1.9	-11.7	5.0
Mozambique	3.5	8.6	0.9	-1.0	7.5	-4.0	-3.3
Rest of Sub-Saharan Africa	3.7	7.0	1.8	-1.7	5.5	-2.7	0.5
Tanzania	0.3	0.4	0.2	-0.3	-0.1	-0.4	0.3
Uganda	0.5	0.5	0.3	-0.3	-0.2	-0.5	0.3
Zambia	0.3	0.6	0.2	-0.6	0.2	0.6	0.0

TABLE 8 Continued

Region	Unskilled Real Wages	Unskilled Real Wages in Agriculture	Unskilled Real Wages in Non-agricultural Sectors	Real Return to Capital	Real Return to Land	Real Return to Natural Resources	Skilled Real Wages
Unambitious scenario							
High-income countries							
Australia/New Zealand	0.5	1.8	0.4	0.2	0.7	1.4	0.3
Canada	-0.1	1.2	-0.1	0.1	0.8	0.0	-0.1
Developed Asia	0.1	-1.0	0.2	0.2	-2.7	0.0	0.2
European Union	0.0	-0.9	0.1	0.0	-1.0	1.0	0.2
Mexico	-0.1	-0.4	0.0	0.0	-0.2	-0.5	0.1
Rest of OECD	2.6	1.4	2.6	1.4	-0.5	3.7	2.9
Turkey	3.8	2.2	4.1	3.2	-2.3	-6.5	6.8
USA	0.0	0.7	0.0	0.1	0.9	0.0	0.0
Middle-income countries							
Argentina	0.4	1.0	0.3	0.1	0.6	-1.4	0.4
Brazil	0.1	0.8	0.1	0.0	0.8	-0.4	0.1
Caribbean economies	0.3	0.5	0.3	0.3	0.2	-2.1	0.2
Chile	0.2	0.7	0.2	-0.1	0.6	-0.5	0.2
China	0.6	0.8	0.5	-0.2	0.9	-1.2	0.6
Colombia	0.1	0.3	0.0	-0.2	0.2	-0.2	0.0
Developing Asia	0.4	0.4	0.4	0.0	0.2	-0.6	0.4
India	0.4	0.5	0.4	-1.0	0.8	-8.9	1.2
Indonesia	0.5	0.4	0.5	0.0	0.0	0.0	0.4

Malaysia	-1.0	-2.1	-1.0	-3.6	-4.4	-13.6	-0.4
Morocco	0.5	0.7	0.5	-0.3	0.7	-3.4	0.4
Peru	0.0	0.1	0.0	0.1	0.0	-0.9	0.0
Philippines	0.3	0.3	0.4	0.0	0.0	-0.4	0.2
Rest of America	0.3	0.8	0.2	-0.1	0.6	-0.9	0.2
Rest of Middle East and North Africa	0.0	0.3	-0.1	0.0	0.5	0.8	-0.2
Rest of South America	0.2	1.0	0.0	-0.5	1.0	-1.7	-0.3
Rest of the World	0.0	0.3	0.0	-0.1	0.5	-0.4	-0.2
South African Customs Union	0.1	0.6	0.1	0.1	0.5	2.5	0.1
Singapore	0.2	1.6	0.2	0.1	0.0	1.1	0.0
Thailand	0.4	-0.3	0.5	0.0	-1.6	-4.2	0.5
Tunisia	0.3	-0.8	0.6	0.6	-2.2	0.1	1.0
Uruguay	0.3	0.6	0.3	-0.1	0.3	-0.9	0.4
Venezuela	0.0	0.3	-0.1	-0.3	0.5	-2.5	-0.2
Vietnam	1.0	1.0	1.0	0.1	0.7	0.7	1.0
Zimbabwe	0.3	0.8	0.2	0.0	0.9	1.5	0.4
Low-income countries Bangladesh	0.4	0.5	0.4	0.1	0.2	0.2	0.5
Madagascar	0.1	0.4	-0.2	-0.3	0.5	0.5	-0.6
Malawi	4.1	2.8	4.9	6.7	-2.6	-11.2	5.1
Mozambique	0.4	1.2	0.1	-0.2	1.0	-0.1	-1.0
Rest of Sub-Saharan Africa	0.0	0.2	-0.1	-0.3	0.0	0.1	-0.2
Tanzania	0.3	0.4	0.3	-0.1	-0.1	0.1	0.4
Uganda	0.4	0.4	0.2	-0.2	-0.1	-0.5	0.3
Zambia	0.4	0.6	0.2	-0.5	0.3	0.4	0.1

Source: Authors' calculations.

On the contrary unskilled labour draws more benefits from partial liberalisation than from full liberalisation in China, India, Morocco, Philippines, Tunisia, Bangladesh, Madagascar, Sub-Saharan Africa and Zambia. The ambitious scenario gives, for example, larger gains for agricultural unskilled labour in these countries than full liberalisation.

The first set of countries benefit initially from a large agricultural trade surplus while countries from the second group have a deficit or a small surplus. Under the two Doha scenarios special and differentiated treatment is applied and allows for reduced liberalisation in agriculture by developing countries: the unambitious scenario even exempts LDCs from any liberalisation in agriculture or manufacturing. As a consequence, import competition increases less and productive factors attached to import-competing sectors faces less downward pressure on remuneration than under full trade liberalisation. In the case of free trade, import competition is increased but this is more than fully offset in the first set of countries by exports-driven activity in agricultural sectors: productive factors attached to these sectors benefit from full trade reform. In the second set of countries full trade liberalisation increases import competition in agricultural sectors, while exports are especially increasing in industrial sectors, so unskilled real wages in agriculture rise more (or fall less) with the partial reforms.

Of course the previous mechanisms do not consider maximisation of national real income and accompanying redistributive policies. Higher national incomes achieved by full liberalisation, or under the ambitious versus unambitious Doha scenario, allows options for poverty reduction beyond those associated directly with remuneration of those production factors owned by poor households.

5. CONCLUDING REMARKS

We have presented an analysis of a potential ambitious versus an unambitious Doha Round outcome. Our simulations are based on negotiating proposals by the US and EU from the run-up to the Hong Kong ministerial meeting in December 2005 around which agreement was not reached when the negotiations were suspended in July 2006. We compared the outcomes from our two Doha scenarios with the estimated effects of full global trade liberalisation.

The results for the Doha scenarios demonstrate the high stakes that remain over completion of this negotiation given the positions articulated by the countries involved. A successful round could deliver real gains both globally and for developing countries. However, the magnitude of those gains depends on the shape of the agreement. A cooperative reform outcome based on the most ambitious components of the December 2005 negotiating proposals of the US and EU delivers noticeably greater benefits than an unambitious outcome based on the lower-end elements of their proposals. The details matter in the differing proposals, such as the tariff and domestic support reduction formulae, tariff caps and number of sensitive and special products. If the Doha Round can be resuscitated, negotiating commitment and diligence will be needed to avoid a shallow outcome given the technical character of these details.

Developing countries are heterogeneous in terms of their own policies, the trade barriers they face and their net agricultural trade. Overall, developing countries gain most – and might achieve the best deal in the negotiations – when they join in the reform process for a global trade agreement. Attention is needed in the case of some of the LDCs and other poor countries that may face declining terms of trade because of higher world agricultural prices or eroding preferences. In addition, many developing countries can achieve the full benefits of trade only with substantial attention to broad development needs that will enhance their competitiveness. This too needs to be part of a successful Doha Round outcome.

REFERENCES

Anderson, J. E. and P. Neary (1999), 'The Mercantilist Index of Trade Policy', NBER Working Paper No. 6870.

Anderson, J. E. and P. Neary (2004), 'Welfare versus Market Access: The Implications of Tariff Structure for Tariff Reform' (http://fmwww.bc.edu/ec-p/wp601.pdf).

Anderson, K. and W. Martin (2005), 'Agricultural Trade Reform and the Doha Development Agenda', *The World Economy*, **28**, 9, 1301–27.

Anderson, K., W. Martin and D. Van der Mensbrugghe (2005a), 'Market and Welfare Implications of Doha Reform Scenarios', in K. Anderson and W. Martin (eds.), *Trade Reform and the Doha Agenda* (Washington, DC: The World Bank).

Anderson, K., W. Martin and D. Van der Mensbrugghe (2005b), 'Doha Merchandise Trade Reform: What's at Stake for Developing Countries?', Plenary Paper for the 8th Annual Conference on Global Trade Analysis, Lubeck, 9–11 June (Washington, DC: The World Bank).

Bchir, M. H., Y. Decreux, J.-L. Guerin and S. Jean (2002), 'Mirage, a General Equilibrium Model for Trade Policy Analysis', CEPII Working Paper No. 2002-17 (CEPII).

Bchir, M. H., L. Fontagne and S. Jean (2005), 'From Bound Duties to Actual Protection: Industrial Protection in the Doha Round', CEPII Working Paper No. 2005-12 (CEPII).

Bouët, A., J.-C. Bureau, Y. Decreux and S. Jean (2005), 'Multilateral Agricultural Trade Liberalisation: The Contrasting Fortunes of Developing Countries in the Doha Round', *The World Economy*, **28**, 9, 1329–54.

Bouët, A., Y. Decreux, L. Fontagné, S. Jean and D. Laborde (2005a), 'Tariff Duties in GTAP6: The MacMap-HS6 Database, Sources and Methodology', in B. V. Dimaranan and R. A. McDougall (eds.), *Global Trade, Assistance and Production: The GTAP 6 Data Base* (Purdue University Centre for Global Trade Analysis).

Bouët, A., Y. Decreux, L. Fontagné, S. Jean and D. Laborde (2005b), 'A Consistent, Ad Valorem Equivalent Measure of Applied Protection Across the World: the MacMap-HS6 Database', CEPII Working Paper No. 2004-22 (CEPII).

Bouët, A., S. Mevel and D. Orden (2006), 'Two Opportunities to Deliver on the Doha Development Pledge', International Food Policy Research Institute (IFPRI) Research Brief No. 6 (July).

Dimaranan, B. (2006), *Global Trade Assistance and Production: The GTAP 6 Data Base* (Purdue University, Centre for Global Trade Analysis, Purdue University).

Fontagne, L., J.-L. Guerin and S. Jean (2005), 'Market Access Liberalisation in the Doha Round: Scenarios and Assessment', *The World Economy*, **28**, 8, 1073–94.

Francois, J., H. Van Meijl and F. Van Tongeren (2005), 'Trade Liberalisation in the Doha Development Round', *Economic Policy*, **20**, 42, 349–91.

Harrison, G., T. Rutherford and D. Tarr (1997), 'Quantifying the Uruguay Round', *Economic Journal*, **107**, 444, 1405–30.

Jean, S., D. Laborde and W. Martin (2005), 'Consequences of Alternative Formulas for Agricultural Tariff Cuts', in K. Anderson and W. Martin (eds.), *Trade Reform and the Doha Agenda* (Washington, DC: The World Bank).

Van der Mensbrugghe, D. (2006), 'Why Numbers Change', in R. Newfarmer (ed.), *Trade, Doha and Development: A Window into the Issues* (Washington, DC: The World Bank).

5

The World Trade Organisation's Doha Cotton Initiative: A Tale of Two Issues

Kym Anderson and Ernesto Valenzuela

1. INTRODUCTION

𝔉OR many developing countries, especially in Africa and Central Asia, cotton is an important cash crop. It is receiving attention of late because four poor cotton-exporting West African countries (the Cotton-4: Benin, Burkina Faso, Chad and Mali) have demanded that cotton subsidy and import tariff removal be part of the World Trade Organisation's Doha Development Agenda (DDA). Cotton subsidies are mostly provided by governments in high-income countries, and part of the US cotton subsidy programme has been ruled illegal following a WTO dispute settlement case brought by Brazil. Hence some reform can be expected soon, especially if the DDA is to live up to its name of being a development round (Sumner, 2006).

This paper seeks to provide estimates of what is at stake in terms of cotton production, trade and economic welfare in African and other developing countries. Specifically, how much would Sub-Saharan Africa gain from removal of all cotton subsidies and tariffs relative to removal of such distortions to other merchandise trade globally? How would the welfare of cotton-importing developing countries with export interests in textiles and clothing be affected by such reform? What would be the relative contributions of different countries' policies – and of domestic supports, export subsidies and import tariffs – to the global gains from removal of those measures? And how would the gains from full reform compare

The authors are grateful for discussions with John Baffes and helpful comments from seminar participants including Larry Hinkle, Elke Kreuzwieser, Will Masters, Maurice Schiff and the editor and two anonymous referees, and for funding from the UK's Department for International Development and the Bank-Netherlands Partnership Programme. This paper is a product of two World Bank research projects, on *Agricultural Trade Reform and the Doha Development Agenda* and *Distortions to Agricultural Incentives*.

91

with the gains that could be expected if and when (a) the US complies with its WTO obligations as laid out in the WTO's dispute settlement Panel and Appellate Body reports (WTO, 2004b and 2005a) and (b) the partial reforms proposed in the Hong Kong Trade Ministerial meeting in December 2005 are implemented as part of the DDA?

The Cotton Initiative under the WTO's DDA has not only the trade policy reform component but also a development component (WTO, 2004a and 2004c). The latter is aimed at boosting the international competitiveness of cotton producers in low-income (especially West African) cotton-exporting countries. One prospective way to do that is for governments of those countries to allow the adoption of new varieties of cotton emerging from the biotechnology revolution, the affordability of which will be greater in the absence of cotton market distortions. We therefore compare the estimated gains from cotton subsidy and tariff reform with the prospective gain from wider adoption by developing countries of genetically modified (GM) cotton, and also ask: how much greater would be the gains to cotton-producing developing countries from GM cotton adoption if global cotton markets were not distorted by subsidies and tariffs? Our results suggest that these trade and technology policy reforms would reinforce each other in terms of gains to developing country farmers.

After presenting a brief background to the world's cotton market in Section 2, this paper seeks to address these questions by using a well-received model of global economy known as GTAP (developed by Purdue University's Global Trade Analysis Project) and a slight modification of database (Version 6.1) of its related trade and protection database, described in Section 3. Empirical simulation results are presented in Section 4 for full trade and subsidy reform and in Section 5 for partial cotton policy reform either by the US in response to the WTO dispute settlement case brought against it by Brazil or as proposed at the Hong Kong Trade Ministerial of the DDA. These are then compared in Section 6 with the estimated effects of GM cotton adoption by various country groups. The paper concludes with a summary of findings and draws out implications for developing country negotiators in the WTO's Doha Round.

2. BACKGROUND: THE GLOBAL COTTON MARKET

Cotton production is highly concentrated in several respects. One is that most production is in a few countries: as of 2005/06, nearly half is produced by just China and the United States, and that rises to more than two-thirds when India and Pakistan are added and to more than three-quarters when Brazil and Ukbekistan are included. Also highly concentrated are exports of cotton lint, with the US, Australia, Uzbekistan and Brazil accounting for almost two-thirds of the world's exports, while the cotton-four in West Africa and the other four countries in

Central Asia bring that total to almost four-fifths (Anderson and Valenzuela, 2006, Appendix Tables A1 and A2). Both production of cotton and its export patterns are distorted very considerably by subsidies to both as well as by tariffs on cotton, textiles and clothing imports (the size of which are shown in Table 1).

Cotton production is also concentrated in the sense that a number of low-income countries depend heavily on cotton for earning foreign exchange. This is especially true of several countries in Sub-Saharan Africa (Benin, Burkina Faso, Chad and Mali) and in Uzbekistan where cotton accounts for more than one-fifth of merchandise exports and, for another six countries in those regions, cotton's share is between 5 and 12 per cent. In 2002 all but three of those eleven African and Central Asian countries had average per capita incomes of less than 80 US cents per day (Table 2). And since much of their cotton production is exported, they compete directly in international markets with highly subsidised exports from the United States.

Cotton usage, on the other hand, is distributed across countries roughly in proportion to their volumes of textile production.[1] Because of high domestic usage by exporters of textiles and clothing in developing Asian countries (and Mexico because of its preferential access to the US and Canadian markets under NAFTA), even relatively large cotton producers such as China, Pakistan and India (see column 1 of Table 3) export only a small fraction of their crop, in contrast to Sub-Saharan Africa where textile production is relatively minor. This explains the pattern of net exports of cotton and textiles across regions (columns 2 and 3 of Table 3), an understanding of which is helpful in explaining the signs of the welfare effects of the technology and policy shocks considered below.

3. THE GTAP MODEL AND DATABASE

The standard Global Trade Analysis Project (GTAP) model of the global economy is used to provide insights into the likely effects of reforming cotton subsidy and trade policies globally and of governments allowing GM cotton technology adoption in some countries without and then with cotton trade and subsidy policy reform globally. The GTAP model (see Hertel, 1997, for comprehensive documentation) is a neoclassical multi-regional, static, applied general equilibrium model that assumes perfect competition, constant returns to scale and unchanging aggregate employment of all factors of production. We use Version 6.1 of the GTAP database (Dimaranan, 2006), which draws on global economic structures, policies and trade flows of 2001. The GTAP model has been aggregated to depict the global economy as having 27 sectors and 39 regions (to highlight

---

[1] That usage pattern has been distorted considerably by import tariffs on textiles and clothing, even after the removal by the end of 2004 of quotas restricting exports of those products from developing countries.

TABLE 1

Cotton Subsidies and Import Tariffs in 2001, and Average Applied Tariffs on Textile and Clothing Imports in 2005[a]

	Cotton Production Subsidies		Cotton Export Subsidies (Per cent)	Cotton Import Tariffs (Per cent)	Textile Import Tariffs (Per cent)	Clothing Import Tariffs (Per cent)
	US$m	Per Cent				
High-income countries	**3,461**	**33.8**	**0.0**	**0.2**	**6.3**	**8.6**
Australia	27	2.2	0.0	0.0	11.6	22.0
United States	2,969	40.2	0.0	0.6	7.3	9.4
EU25	430	39.3	0.0	0.0	6.4	7.9
Eastern Europe and C. Asia	**153**	**2.3**	**0.0**	**0.1**	**8.8**	**16.6**
East Asia and Pacific	**0**	**0.0**	**0.0**	**2.0**	**9.7**	**15.5**
China	0	0.0	0.0	2.8	8.9	15.7
South Asia	**235**	**2.9**	**0.0**	**3.8**	**20.8**	**20.0**
India	235	4.4	0.0	7.0	26.2	18.9
Middle East and North Africa	**26**	**0.9**	**2.4**	**6.1**	**16.2**	**21.4**
Sub-Saharan Africa	**1**	**0.1**	**0.0**	**6.3**	**10.6**	**18.5**
Latin America and Caribbean	**36**	**1.5**	**0.0**	**4.1**	**10.5**	**17.2**
Brazil	9	1.3	0.0	3.8	11.7	14.8
Mexico	25	4.5	0.0	9.9	13.5	20.8

Note:

[a] GTAP database Version 6.1, with tariffs updated to 2005 following phase-out of textile and clothing quotas, and assuming a cotton output subsidy in the US of 40 per cent in 2001.

Source: Update of GTAP database Version 6.1 at www.gtap.org.

TABLE 2

Dependence of Cotton-producing Developing Countries on Cotton Export Earnings, Average 2000–02

	Share of Total Merchandise Export Revenue from Cotton (Per cent)	Value of Cotton Exports (US$m)	National Share of Global Value of Cotton Exports (Per cent)	Cumulative Share of Global Value of Cotton Exports (Per cent)	Per Capita Income (US$)
Benin	46.8	131	1.9	1.9	380
Burkina Faso	37.2	94	1.4	3.3	250
Chad	32.9	59	0.9	4.2	210
Uzbekistan	23.8	747	11.1	15.3	310
Mali	22.4	161	2.4	17.7	240
Tajikistan	12.3	89	1.3	19.0	180
Togo	9.1	35	0.5	19.5	270
Turkmenistan	7.6	201	3.0	22.5	1,120
Kyrgyzstan	6.7	33	0.5	23.0	290
Zimbabwe	6.3	133	2.0	25.0	<700
World	**0.1**	**6,656**	**100.0**	**100.0**	**5,510**

Source: FAOSTAT database at www.fao.org, except for final column which is from the World Bank's *World Development Indicators 2004* for the year 2002.

TABLE 3

Cotton Net Farm Income and Net Export Positions in 2001, and Impact of Removing Cotton Subsidies and Tariffs[a] on Cotton Output, Exports, Net Farm Income and Economic Welfare
(Per cent and 2001 US$m)

	Index of Cotton Production Specialisation[c]	Net Exports[b] ($b) of:		Change in Cotton Output Volume (Per cent)	Change in Value Added in Cotton Production (Per cent)	Change in Value of Cotton Exports (Per cent)	Welfare Change ($m):	
		Cotton	Textiles and Clothing				Total	That Due to Terms of Trade Change
High-income countries	**0.3**	**1.0**	**-92.0**	**-20**	**-15**	**-18**	**465**	**275**
Australia	3.2	1.1	-2.6	25	22	38	137	125
United States	0.7	2.2	-60.7	-25	-18	-29	429	443
EU25	0.1	-1.0	-28.8	-54	-53	-49	14	-109
Developing countries	**3.8**	**-1.0**	**92.0**	**6**	**4**	**46**	**-182**	**-275**
E. Europe and C. Asia	4.3	0.3	7.4	7	3	36	-14	-36
East Asia	3.0	-1.4	60.4	2	2	72	-83	-127
China	4.8	-0.1	41.9	2	2	76	50	45
South Asia	**14.5**	**-1.0**	**24.5**	**2**	**1**	**55**	**-96**	**-99**
Bangladesh	12.7	-0.3	3.8	8	5	68	-11	-21
India	12.8	-0.6	11.9	-1	0	31	-85	-79
Pakistan	29.1	-0.1	6.8	5	3	61	-7	-5
M. East & North Africa	**2.2**	**0.4**	**-3.3**	**6**	**6**	**37**	**19**	**26**
Sub-Saharan Africa	**5.8**	**1.1**	**-1.8**	**32**	**31**	**55**	**147**	**113**
Southern and East Africa	2.3	0.2	0.5	19	19	43	22	16
Western Africa	7.3	0.8	-2.3	38	36	60	125	97
Latin America and Car.	**1.1**	**-0.4**	**4.8**	**11**	**9**	**54**	**-155**	**-152**
Brazil	1.2	0.1	-0.0	10	10	58	13	12
Mexico	0.7	-0.5	4.0	13	11	42	-128	-136
World	**1.0**	**0.0**	**0.0**	**-1**	**-2**	**8**	**283**	**0**

Notes:

[a] Removal of those distortions left after the phase-out of the quotas at the end of 2004.

[b] Exports minus imports, both valued at f.o.b. prices as in the GTAP database 6.05.

[c] Cotton's national share in GDP relative to the global share. In the GTAP database the sector is 'plant-based fibres' and so includes such products as flax (important only for Bangladesh in the above countries).

Source: Authors' GTAP model simulation results.

the main participants in the world's cotton markets, two of which are newly disaggregated countries: Nigeria and Pakistan). Trade is modelled using a nested Armington structure in which aggregate import demand for each sector's product is the outcome of allocating domestic absorption between domestic goods and aggregate imports, and then aggregate import demand is allocated across source countries to determine the bilateral trade flows.

Two modifications have been made to the structure of protection in Version 6.1 of the GTAP database. One relates to cotton subsidies in the United States. In Version 6.1, which reflects subsidy notifications to the WTO, the subsidies showing for the US in 2001 are much less than actually paid through its various and complex cotton programmes: $1.0 billion as production subsidies and zero as export subsidies, compared with an average annual total payment of $3.0 billion for the 2000–02 period according to Baffes (2005, Table 4, drawing on official data from the USDA). We therefore adjusted the subsidy rates to raise overall payments to that $3 billion level (of which direct payments and counter-cyclical payments are paid per unit of land, marketing loan benefits and crop insurance subsidies are paid as input subsidies, and coupled output payments plus Step 2 payments to US cotton textile producers and to US cotton exporters, along with export credit guarantees, are paid as production subsidies).[2] The resulting subsidy rates are shown in Table 1, along with information on the (relatively small) tariffs on cotton imports.[3] For the US it amounts to a production subsidy in 2001 of 40 per cent. This may be conservative, as it compares with a recent projection for 2004–06 of 56 per cent with the Step 2 programme intact and 46 per cent if it is repealed without re-instrumentation (Sumner, 2005, Table 3).

The other modification to the GTAP protection database is to take account of the completion of the implementation of the Uruguay Round Agreement on

---

[2] The latter two are export subsidies but, since an export subsidy is equivalent to a production subsidy plus a consumption tax at the same rate, and since US buyers of domestically produced cotton receive a consumption subsidy to compensate for the price-raising effect of the export subsidies on cotton, the two elements in the Step 2 programme sum to the equivalent of just a cotton production subsidy. That programme's payments amounted to one-seventh of total dollars of cotton supports during 2000–02 (Baffes, 2005, Table 4) and, if it were not repealed, would amount to one-sixth during 2004–06 (Sumner, 2005, Table 3). In any case they were found to be illegal recently by the WTO's Dispute Settlement Panel and Appellate Body (WTO, 2004b and 2005a). As a result, on 1 February, 2006, the US Congress agreed to reform both components of the Step 2 programme by 1 August, 2006. How this reform impacts the market depends on the extent of re-instrumentation of that portion of the overall support, as discussed in Section 5 below.

[3] No cotton subsidies are shown for China in the GTAP protection database, even though there have been some in past years. According to Huang et al. (2004), the degree of protection varied from positive to negative during 2001 and the key intervention was an export subsidy. Since then China has committed to zero export subsidies, as part of its WTO accession agreement. Those zero entries in Table 1 are also consistent with the OECD's recent Producer Support Estimates for China (OECD, 2006), which for 2001 show no direct subsidy payments and a slightly negative nominal rate of protection for cotton producers. For an up-to-date assessment of China's cotton policies, see Shui (2005).

TABLE 4

Contribution to National Economic Welfare and Value Added in Cotton Production That Would Result From Removing Cotton Subsidies and Tariffs,[a] by Region and by Policy Instrument

Benefiting Region:	By Reforming Region:					By Policy Instrument:		
	US	EU25	Other High-income Countries	Developing Countries	Total, World	Tariff	Export Subsidy	Domestic Support
Panel A: Equivalent Variation in Income in 2001 US$ Million								
High-income countries	**374**	**109**	**0**	**–17**	**465**	**15**	**–7**	**457**
Australia	109	14	8	6	137	2	2	134
United States	401	8	1	19	429	18	1	411
EU25	–64	110	–5	–28	14	6	–9	18
Developing countries	**–224**	**22**	**–3**	**24**	**–182**	**13**	**7**	**–204**
E. Europe & C. Asia	–25	2	1	7	–14	1	0	–14
East Asia	–54	–15	–6	–9	–83	–20	–2	–63
China	60	–12	2	–1	50	–13	0	62
South Asia	**–71**	**–5**	**–3**	**–17**	**–96**	**5**	**–1**	**–99**
India	–57	–6	–1	–20	–85	0	0	–84
M. East & Nth Africa	**8**	**–4**	**1**	**14**	**19**	**1**	**8**	**10**
Sub-Saharan Africa	**72**	**33**	**4**	**39**	**147**	**32**	**2**	**112**
Latin America & Car.	**–154**	**9**	**0**	**–10**	**–155**	**–6**	**0**	**–150**
Brazil	6	6	0	1	13	0	0	12
World	**149**	**130**	**–4**	**7**	**283**	**28**	**0**	**253**

Panel B: Per Cent Change in Value Added

High-income countries	**-12.9**	**-3.2**	**-0.4**	**1.2**	**-15.4**	**0.4**	**0.1**	**-15.9**
Australia	22.4	2.5	-4.2	1.5	22.2	0.2	0.3	21.6
United States	-20.1	1.0	0.3	0.9	-17.9	0.3	0.1	-18.3
EU25	8.6	-66.2	0.4	3.9	-53.3	2.3	0.5	-56.1
Developing countries	**3.8**	**1.3**	**0.1**	**-0.9**	**4.3**	**-0.2**	**-0.1**	**4.6**
E. Europe and C. Asia	**3.3**	**2.3**	**0.1**	**-2.4**	**3.3**	**0.0**	**0.1**	**3.1**
East Asia	**1.4**	**0.5**	**0.1**	**-0.1**	**1.9**	**-0.2**	**0.0**	**2.0**
China	1.1	0.5	0.0	-0.1	1.5	-0.2	0.0	1.7
South Asia	**1.9**	**0.3**	**0.1**	**-1.6**	**0.7**	**-0.7**	**0.0**	**1.4**
India	1.7	0.2	0.0	-2.4	-0.4	-1.1	0.0	0.7
M. East and Nth Africa	**5.7**	**3.4**	**0.3**	**-3.2**	**6.1**	**-0.8**	**-1.9**	**8.8**
Sub-Saharan Africa	**16.0**	**6.6**	**0.8**	**7.1**	**30.6**	**5.1**	**0.5**	**24.8**
Latin America and Car.	**9.6**	**1.3**	**0.2**	**-1.8**	**9.4**	**-1.1**	**0.1**	**10.4**
Brazil	8.0	2.5	0.3	-0.5	10.3	0.3	0.2	9.9
World	**-1.4**	**-0.1**	**0.0**	**-0.2**	**-1.8**	**0.0**	**0.0**	**-1.8**

Note:

[a] Removal of those distortions left after the eventual phase-out of the quotas under the Multifibre Agreement at the end of 2004.

Source: Authors' GTAP model simulation results.

Textiles and Clothing by the end of 2004, at which time all trade-restricting quotas were abolished and were replaced by a tariff-only regime. We then recalibrate the model's baseline by implementing that protection change, and the change in US cotton subsidy rates, before running the simulations described below.[4]

4. THE GLOBAL COST OF COTTON SUBSIDIES AND TARIFFS

What is the cost of current distortions to cotton markets or, equivalently, what would be the effects of eliminating all cotton subsidies and import tariffs, as called for by African cotton-exporting countries as part of the WTO's Doha Development Agenda? Given the extent of subsidies to cotton production and exports, and of tariffs on cotton imports as of 2001 (modified as described in the previous section), we estimate using the GTAP model that their removal would boost global economic welfare by $283 million per year,[5] and would raise the price of cotton in international markets by an average of 12.9 per cent.[6] The price rise ensures that all cotton-exporting countries would benefit, while net importers of cotton would be worse off, as shown in the right-hand columns of Table 3.

What is striking about the welfare effects is their distribution among developing countries (Table 3 and Figure 1). Especially noteworthy is the relatively large benefit bestowed on Sub-Saharan Africa, of $147 million per year. About two-fifths of that would go to the Cotton-4 and another one-fifth to other West African countries. This is driven by an estimated increase in Sub-Saharan African cotton output and value added in cotton production (net farm income) of nearly one-third, and in the real value of the region's cotton exports of more than 50 per cent. By contrast, cotton output and exports would fall by one-quarter in the United States and would halve in the EU (middle columns of Table 3). That would raise Sub-Saharan Africa's share of global cotton exports from 12 to 17 per cent, and the share of all developing countries from 52 to 72 per cent.

---

[4] US and other cotton subsidy programmes have been the subject of intense analysis in recent years, although mostly by partial rather than general equilibrium modellers. For reviews of that literature, see FAO (2004), Baffes (2005) and Sumner (2006).

[5] Of course if textile and clothing tariffs were also removed, global welfare would increase far more: by an extra $6.8 billion per year, according to our GTAP model results.

[6] This is almost identical to the 12.6 per cent claimed by Brazil using a model developed by FAPRI (FAPRI, 2005) and close to the 10 per cent estimated by Sumner (2006, p. 282), which is also the simple average of the studies surveyed by Baffes (2005, p. 122), although the range reported by Baffes is up to 30 per cent. When we alter the GTAP trade elasticities to the larger ones used in the World Bank's Linkage model (see van der Mensbrugghe, 2005), our estimate of 12.9 per cent falls to 11.9 per cent.

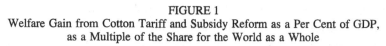

FIGURE 1
Welfare Gain from Cotton Tariff and Subsidy Reform as a Per Cent of GDP,
as a Multiple of the Share for the World as a Whole

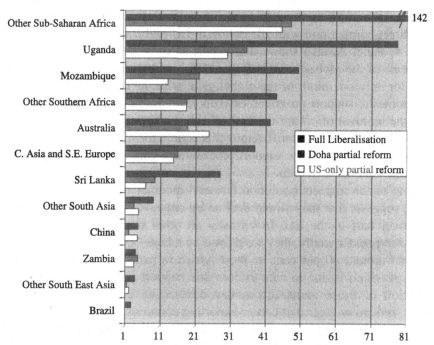

Source: Authors' GTAP model simulation results.

Also striking is a comparison of the welfare result from cotton reform with
that from removing *all* merchandise tariffs and agricultural subsidies. While the
latter gain is nearly 300 times as great as the former globally, for Sub-Saharan
Africa cotton reform is crucial: its potential contribution to the region's welfare
of $147 million per year is one-fifth of the estimated $733 million gain for the
region from the freeing of *all* goods markets globally, according to our GTAP
model results. It is therefore not surprising that some African trade negotiators
have threatened to walk out of the WTO's Doha Round of talks if substantial
reforms to cotton policies are not included in the final Doha agreement – in which
case the global cost of not reforming cotton would be many times greater than
implied in Table 3.

If the distortions to cotton markets were removed, the final row of Table 4,
Panel A, shows that the United States' policy reform would be responsible for
more than half of the global gain. Perhaps more surprising is the result that the
EU25 is responsible for nearly all of the rest, but that is mainly because the cost
of the EU's policies to its own economy is so high. Even so, the estimated cost

to Sub-Saharan Africa is only half due to US policies and only one-quarter to developing countries' policies, with most of the rest due to EU cotton policies. The reason the latter are so much more important to Sub-Saharan Africa has to do with the pattern of bilateral trade in cotton, as Sub-Saharan African cotton is sold in direct competition with EU cotton in EU and East Asian markets.

Table 4, Panel A, also shows that export subsidy removal would contribute almost none of the global benefits from reform, and cotton tariff removal would account for only one-ninth of the global gain, with the other eight-ninths due to cutting domestic support programmes. This latter result contrasts markedly with that for the removal of *all* agricultural subsidies and tariffs (to which cotton is a tiny contributor), whereby tariff removal accounts for a huge 93 per cent of the global benefits and domestic support programmes only five per cent (Anderson, Martin and Valenzuela, 2006).

Turning to the impacts on cotton farmers' incomes of such reform, Table 4, Panel B, suggests that they would decline by one-sixth in the United States and by just over half in the EU. In virtually all other regions, however, they are estimated to rise. Crucially, they would rise by a huge 30 per cent in Sub-Saharan Africa and around 40 per cent in West Africa in particular – more than three-quarters of which is due to cuts to domestic support programmes. The relative distribution of those gains across key developing countries is depicted in Figure 2. It is no wonder that cotton-exporting countries in Africa are calling for large cuts to those subsidies as part of the Cotton Initiative within the WTO's Doha Development Agenda (DDA), and for assistance to increase their cotton productivity and responsiveness to higher export prices.

5. PROSPECTIVE GAINS FROM PARTIAL REFORM OF COTTON SUBSIDIES AND TARIFFS

While the full reform results presented above are not likely to materialise in the immediate future, they provide a useful benchmark against which to compare the estimated effects of partial reforms. In this section we consider two partial reform scenarios: liberalisation in the United States alone, as a possible response to the outcome of the WTO dispute settlement case brought against it by Brazil; and a broader liberalisation consistent with what was agreed at the Hong Kong Trade Ministerial in December 2005 as part of the DDA.

a. US-only Partial Reform Following the WTO Dispute Settlement Case

How much cotton reform can be expected in the United States as a result of the US being found not in compliance with its WTO obligations, as laid out in the WTO's dispute settlement Panel and Appellate Body reports (WTO, 2004b and

FIGURE 2

Percentage Change in Value Added in Cotton Production from Reform of Cotton Tariffs
and Subsidies, as a Multiple of the Percentage Change for Developing Countries as a Whole

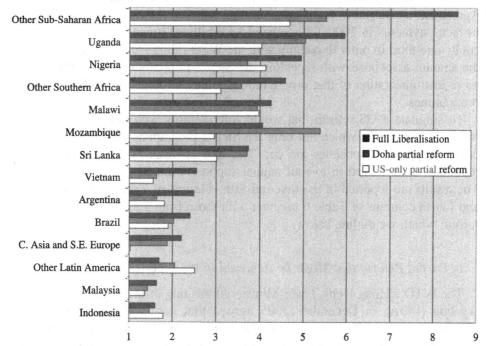

Source: Authors' GTAP model simulation results.

2005a)? The reports ruled that the Step 2 programme and the export credit guarantees
were prohibited export subsidies and domestic-content subsidies. They also ruled
that all US cotton production subsidies are not minimally trade-distorting and so
should be in the amber box rather than the green box (to use the terminology of
the Uruguay Round Agreement on Agriculture). On the first, the US already has
agreed to repeal the two parts of its Step 2 programme (passed by the US Congress
on 1 February, 2006). That programme provided an export subsidy to cotton
producers and a consumption subsidy to US users of domestically produced
cotton (the sum of which in economic terms is equivalent to a production subsidy
of the same rate). At one extreme, if those dollars of support to US cotton farmers
through the Step 2 programme are completely re-instrumented to direct production
subsidies, there would be effectively no global market impact of that repeal. At
the other extreme, if there was zero re-instrumentation and the total expenditure
on cotton support was reduced by the full amount of the Step 2 payments, this
would be equivalent in 2000–02 to a one-seventh reduction in the aggregate
subsidy to US cotton production.

Turning to the second part of the WTO ruling, if US cotton producer subsidies are now to be counted as part of the country's amber box measures, they should not exceed the support provided in 1992 (the limit year under the Uruguay Round Agreement on Subsidies and Countervailing Measures), which was $2.0 billion. In fact, payments in 2000–02 averaged $3.0 billion, suggesting they should be cut by one-third in order to comply with the WTO ruling – or by more than twice the amount associated with repealing the Step 2 programme even if there were no re-instrumentation of that programme's dollars to domestic producer support programmes.

To simulate a US reform that would fully comply with those WTO rulings, we ran a scenario in which not only the Step 2 programme is removed but also domestic producer subsidies are cut. The sum of these two is equivalent to a reduction by one-third in overall annual support, from $3 billion to $2 billion. The results are reported in the first and fifth columns of Table 5, and in the first and fourth columns of Table 6 together with those from a more-extensive partial reform which we outline below.

b. Partial Reform that Might be Achieved in the WTO's Doha Round

The WTO's Hong Kong Trade Ministerial meeting of the Doha Development Agenda (DDA) in December 2005 agreed that cotton export subsidies be eliminated during 2006, that least-developed countries get duty-free access for their cotton exports to high-income countries by the time implementation of the DDA commences, and that domestic cotton subsidies be reduced faster and more ambitiously than other agricultural domestic support programmes during DDA implementation (WTO, 2005b). How far might that go towards yielding the potential gains to low-income countries from full reform as reported above? To address this question, we ran another partial liberalisation scenario in which we:

- remove all cotton export subsidies globally,
- remove tariffs on imports by all high-income countries (HICs) of cotton from pertinent UN-defined least-developed countries (LDCs, comprising South Asia excluding India, Pakistan and Sri Lanka plus Sub-Saharan Africa excluding Nigeria and the Southern African Customs Union in terms of our regions),[7] and

---

[7] For the list of LDCs, see http://www.un.org/special-rep/ohrlls/ldc/list.htm. Due to regional aggregations in the GTAP dataset we use, our Sub-Saharan African group has some non-LDCs (including Zimbabwe, although it – like the three poorest Central Asian nations – probably now qualifies as an LDC) while LDCs in other regions are not so classified because they are too small a part of 'rest of region x' categories.

TABLE 5

Impact of US and Doha Partial Reform of Cotton Subsidies and Tariffs on Economic Welfare and Net Incomes of Cotton Farmers, by Region

(Equivalent variation in income in 2001 US$m, and per cent change in value added)

	Change in Economic Welfare ($m)				Change in Value Added (Per cent)			
	Compliance by US to WTO DS Panel[b]	Doha Partial Reform[a]		Full Reform	Compliance by US to WTO DS Panel[b]	Doha Partial Reform[a]		Full Reform
		Due to Trade Measures	Total			Due to Trade Measures	Total	
High-income countries	**210**	**−9**	**280**	**465**	**−4.1**	**0.1**	**−5.4**	**−15.4**
Australia	33	1	41	137	7.7	0.3	7.5	22.2
United States	229	0	231	429	−6.6	0.1	−6.0	−17.9
EU25	−29	−9	42	14	4.2	0.6	−20.9	−53.3
Japan	3	−1	−4	−24	1.1	0	0.5	1.5
Developing countries	**−94**	**7**	**−88**	**−182**	**1.2**	**−0.1**	**1.7**	**4.3**
E. Europe & C. Asia	−10	0	−12	−14	1.1	0.1	2.1	3.3
East Asia	−23	−2	−33	−83	0.5	0	0.7	1.9
China	19	0	15	50	0.4	0	0.6	1.5
South Asia	**−31**	**−1**	**−36**	**−96**	**0.7**	**0**	**0.9**	**0.7**
Bangladesh	−5	0	−6	−11	1.1	0.1	1.3	5.0
India	−23	0	−27	−85	0.6	0	0.7	−0.4
Pakistan	−4	−1	−5	−7	0.8	0.1	1.0	3.0
M. East & North Africa	**2**	**7**	**8**	**19**	**1.8**	**−1.7**	**1.3**	**6.1**
Sub-Saharan Africa	**20**	**3**	**35**	**147**	**5.0**	**0.6**	**8.2**	**30.6**
Southern and East Africa	4	0	6	22	3.7	0.3	6.3	18.8
Western Africa	16	3	29	125	5.6	0.7	9.2	35.7
Latin America & Car.	**−52**	**0**	**−50**	**−155**	**3.0**	**0.1**	**3.6**	**9.4**
Brazil	0	0	2	13	2.3	0.2	3.4	10.3
Mexico	−35	0	−36	−128	4.1	0	4.4	10.5
World	**116**	**−2**	**192**	**283**	**−0.4**	**0**	**−0.5**	**−1.8**

Notes:

[a] 'Trade measures' consist of removal of all export subsidies and removal of tariffs on high-income countries' imports of cotton from LDCs; 'Total' adds a one-third cut in domestic support in high-income countries.

[b] Reduction by one-third in cotton production subsidies (average 2000–02) in US alone.

Source: Authors' GTAP model simulation results.

TABLE 6

Impact of US and Doha Partial Reform of Cotton Subsidies and Tariffs on Cotton Production Volume and Real Value of Exports, by Region

(Per cent)

	Change in Output Volume (Per cent)			Change in Value of Exports (Per cent)		
	Compliance by US to WTO DS Panel[a]	Doha Partial Reform	Full Reform	Compliance by US to WTO DS Panel[a]	Doha Partial Reform	Full Reform
High-income countries	**-5.3**	**-7.7**	**-20.4**	**-3.9**	**-6.6**	**-18.2**
Australia	8.6	8.3	25.0	11.8	12.3	38.1
United States	-9.7	-8.9	-24.6	-11.8	-9.7	-29.0
EU25	4.4	-21.7	-54.0	6.1	-18.5	-48.8
Japan	1.1	0.3	0.7	13.5	11.8	61.9
Developing countries	**1.5**	**2.1**	**5.7**	**8.5**	**12.8**	**46.3**
E. Europe & C. Asia	1.3	2.9	7.0	5.5	12.5	35.9
East Asia	0.6	0.8	2.4	14.1	18.8	71.9
China	0.5	0.7	2.0	17.4	21.6	75.7
South Asia	**1.1**	**1.4**	**1.7**	**9.5**	**13.7**	**54.7**
Bangladesh	1.7	2.1	8.1	8.0	11.2	67.5
India	1.0	1.2	-0.6	9.0	13.2	31.1
Pakistan	1.2	1.6	4.7	11.7	16.5	60.6
M. East & North Africa	**1.8**	**1.3**	**6.2**	**9.1**	**7.1**	**37.4**
Sub-Saharan Africa	**5.2**	**8.6**	**32.0**	**8.6**	**14.2**	**55.0**
Southern and East Africa	3.8	6.4	19.4	7.9	13.1	42.4
Western Africa	5.8	9.7	38.0	8.8	14.7	59.2
Latin America & Car.	**3.5**	**4.3**	**11.0**	**15.3**	**15.7**	**54.0**
Brazil	2.2	3.3	9.8	11.0	16.7	57.6
Mexico	5.3	5.1	13.0	13.4	14.4	42.3
World	**-0.2**	**-0.3**	**-0.8**	**1.1**	**1.3**	**7.9**

Note:

[a] Reduction of one-third in production subsidies (average 2000–02) in US alone.

Source: Authors' GTAP model simulation results.

• reduce by one-third all applied cotton production subsidies in all high-income countries (not just in the US as in the previous partial reform scenario).[8]

c. Comparison of the Two Partial-reform Scenarios with the Full-liberalisation Results

Impacts of this Doha partial reform simulation and the US-only partial reform simulation on regional welfare and on value added in cotton production (net farm income) are reported in Table 5 and in Figures 1 and 2, and the effects on cotton output and exports are shown in Table 6, from which several points are worth stressing.

First, the US-only reform would provide virtually all of the net benefits to the US economy that are generated by the Doha scenario, but only around three-fifths of the estimated net welfare and value-added effects, and two-fifths of the export effects, that Sub-Saharan Africa can expect from Doha cotton reform. Thus while the WTO dispute settlement case is potentially very helpful to non-US cotton producers, at best it is likely to generate barely half the benefits that could come from Doha cotton reform.

Second, by showing there the contributions of trade measures (export subsidy and import tariff reform) separately, it is clear that virtually all the gains from the Doha partial reform would come from reducing domestic producer support programmes. This is not surprising given the earlier results in Table 4 from full reform by instrument, and the knowledge that LDCs already enjoy close to duty-free access to HIC markets through various preference schemes.

Third, while the global welfare gains from the Doha partial reform are two-thirds those from full reform, much of the former would accrue to those cutting their domestic supports, most notably the United States. The overall welfare benefits from the Doha reform simulation to Sub-Saharan Africa and to Central Asia, by contrast, are only one-quarter what they would be from full removal of all cotton programmes. That is also true of the benefits to Sub-Saharan Africa's cotton farmers.

Fourth, Sub-Saharan Africa's cotton output and exports would rise four times as much (and Central Asia's two-and-a-half times as much) under full reform as under the Doha partial reform scenario. If the extent of reduction in applied domestic support to cotton farmers in HICs was less than the one-third assumed here, these differences would be even greater. That is, how much poor African

---

[8] There may also be some reduction in bound cotton tariffs as a result of the non-agricultural market access negotiations, but we ignore that by assuming applied tariffs are sufficiently below bound rates ('binding overhang') for the latter to remain unchanged, which is especially likely in developing countries as they are to be allowed to make lesser cuts than high-income countries (under so-called Special and Differential Treatment, SDT – see Anderson and Martin, 2006). Similarly, because of binding overhang also in domestic subsidies, and SDT, we assume developing countries will not have to lower their cotton production subsidies.

countries and their cotton farmers gain from the DDA Cotton Initiative will hinge crucially on the extent of reform to applied (as distinct from WTO-bound) domestic subsidies.

Finally, what difference would these scenarios make to the average price of cotton in international markets? Under full reform, that average price is estimated to rise by 12.9 per cent, while in the Doha and US-only scenarios it rises by just 4.4 and 3.2 per cent, respectively.

6. WHAT IMPACT WOULD GM COTTON ADOPTION HAVE ON THE GAINS FROM TRADE REFORM?

The Cotton Initiative involves two parts: in addition to trade and subsidy reform, the WTO's General Council has also attached importance to development aspects of the Cotton Initiative, stressing the complementarity between the trade and development components (WTO, 2004a and 2004c). The latter is aimed at boosting the international competitiveness of cotton production in low-income countries. One prospective way to do that is for governments of those countries to allow the adoption of new varieties of cotton emerging from the biotechnology revolution. How do the above estimated gains from cotton subsidy and tariff reform compare with the prospective gains from wider adoption by developing countries of genetically modified (GM) cotton? And how much greater would those gains be to cotton-producing developing countries from GM cotton adoption if global cotton markets were not distorted by subsidies and tariffs, and vice versa?

To simulate the economic effect of adoption of GM cotton, Anderson et al. (2008) assume that total factor productivity (TFP) in cotton production would rise by five per cent in most adopting countries, net of any higher cost of GM seed. This output-augmenting, Hicks-neutral TFP shock is a conservative estimate of the gain to farmers, according to experience to date (Marra et al., 2002; Qaim and Zilberman, 2003; and Huang et al., 2004) and bearing in mind that typically, in a small number of years after GM cotton adoption is allowed, more than four-fifths of production moves to GM varieties. For India and Sub-Saharan Africa other than South Africa, however, a TFP shock of 15 per cent is assumed. Even that higher value is conservative for those countries, according to Qaim and Zilberman (2003), because those countries' yields per hectare with conventional varieties are less than one-third yields in the rest of the world, and the GM field trials in India have been boosting yields by as much as 60 per cent.[9]

---

[9] There are also benefits from insect-resistant Bt cotton in terms of improved health for farmers (see Hossain et al., 2004), and also less pesticide damage to soil and water, but these benefits are ignored in what follows.

Two GM cotton adoption simulations are presented, bearing in mind that by the GTAP model's base year of 2001 the US, Australia and South Africa had fully adopted GM cotton, and China was halfway through its adoption process. The first simulation has China completing its adoption process and all other countries except the rest of Sub-Saharan Africa adopting GM cotton, while in the second simulation Sub-Saharan Africa also adopts.[10]

If all other countries adopt GM cotton, cotton output in the early-adopting countries falls in response to the output expansion in newly adopting regions. If Sub-Saharan Africa continues to procrastinate, its cotton output, net farm income and exports would fall further. By contrast, if Sub-Saharan Africa were also to embrace this technology, its cotton industry would expand more than any other region's, and this would more than make up its losses to 2001 from adoption by the first four adopters (Anderson et al., 2008, Tables 5 and 6).

Even without Sub-Saharan Africa embracing this new biotechnology, global welfare would jump $2.0 billion per year if other countries adopt GM cotton; but adoption by the rest of Africa would raise that global benefit to $2.3 billion, with two-thirds of that extra $0.3 billion being enjoyed by Africa itself. Asia's developing countries that are net importers of cotton gain even if they grow little or no cotton (see columns 1 and 2 of Table 7), because the international price of that crucial input into their textile industry would be lower in these scenarios. With complete catch-up as in the second of these scenarios, the gains to Central Asia, Sub-Saharan Africa and South Asia are 10, 13 and 23 times greater than the global gains when expressed as a percentage of regional GDP (Anderson et al., 2008, Table 6). South Asia's are especially large because it is a large producer *and* user of cotton.

The estimate of the global benefits from full GM cotton adoption by developing countries is eight times larger than the above estimate of the global gain from complete removal of all cotton subsidies and tariffs, and 12 times larger than the global gain from the Doha partial cotton reform simulation. The differences are less marked for Sub-Saharan Africa, but even so its estimated gain from adopting GM cotton varieties is well above that from full removal of all trade-distorting cotton policies and around six times that from the Doha partial reform simulation considered above. And its efficiency gains from GM adoption are more than outweighed by any adverse impact it has on the region's terms of trade even in the presence of trade-distorting policies.

---

[10] The reason it is worth examining separately the impact of adoption by the rest of Sub-Saharan Africa is that the region has a history of very slow adoption of new agricultural technologies in the 1970s and 1980s, and during the 1990s its investments in agricultural R&D grew only one per cent per year and spending actually fell in about half the countries for which data exist (Science Council, 2005). This approach also allows us to address the question of whether efficiency gains from GM adoption in Africa is more than outweighed by any adverse impact it has on the region's terms of trade.

TABLE 7

Prospective Effects of Completing GM Cotton Adoption Globally Post-2001 on National Economic Welfare and Net Cotton Farm Incomes, Without and With Cotton Subsidies and Tariffs Removed

	Without Cotton Subsidy and Tariff Reform		With Cotton Subsidies and Tariffs First Removed, and Then GM Catch-up	With Simultaneous Cotton Subsidy/Tariff Removal and GM Catch-up
	Without SSAfrican GM Adoption	With SSAfrican GM Adoption		
Panel A: Effects on Welfare (US$m) of:				
High-income countries	**318**	**366**	**279**	**744**
Australia	−14	−28	−58	80
United States	61	57	−25	404
Developing countries	**1,701**	**1,957**	**2,043**	**1,866**
E. Europe & C. Asia	325	317	317	303
China	113	100	94	144
Other Southeast Asia	31	63	83	−48
India	817	822	855	771
Other South Asia	147	148	151	140
M. East & North Africa	157	175	211	194
Sub-Saharan Africa	−13	199	223	370
Latin America & Car.	124	135	146	−8
World	**2,018**	**2,323**	**2,322**	**2,610**
Panel B: Effects on Value Added in Cotton Production (Per cent change) in:				
High-income countries	**−2.7**	**−4.5**	**−5.0**	**−19.3**
Australia	−5.6	−9.3	−10.3	9.6
United States	−2.7	−3.9	−3.7	−20.9
Developing countries	**−2.7**	**−2.2**	**−2.2**	**2.0**
E. Europe & C. Asia	−2.3	−3.1	−3.5	−0.3
China	−1.7	−1.9	−2.0	−0.5
Other Southeast Asia	−1.6	−1.9	−2.0	3.1
India	−3.6	−3.9	−4.1	−4.5
Other South Asia	−2.1	−2.5	−2.7	1.8
M. East & North Africa	−2.7	−4.5	−5.2	0.6
Sub-Saharan Africa	−7.2	10.0	9.0	41.6
Latin America & Car.	−1.7	−3.4	−3.7	5.3
World	**−2.7**	**−2.9**	**−2.9**	**−4.6**

Source: Anderson, Valenzuela and Jackson (2008).

Indeed, if all distortions to cotton markets were removed, that global estimate would be virtually no different, for reasons explained in Alston et al. (1988) and Anderson and Nielsen (2004). But the gains to developing countries in the absence of distortionary cotton policies would be slightly greater (12 per cent so in the case of Sub-Saharan Africa), while those to high-income countries would be less (middle columns of Table 7).

Were these two reforms (GM catch-up and subsidy removal) to occur simultaneously, they would reinforce each other in Sub-Saharan Africa as each expands the region's cotton production and exports and so makes the gain from the other change larger. This is evident in the final column of Table 7, which shows that the gain to Sub-Saharan Africa would then be ($223m + $147m =) $370m. This is equivalent to $199m + $172m, the former appearing in column 2 of Table 6 and the latter being the gain to Sub-Saharan Africa from global removal of cotton subsidies and tariffs had GM catch-up occurred before that reform. Also, by comparing the final columns of Tables 5 and 7, and Figures 1 and 3, it is evident that while numerous cotton-importing developing countries lose from subsidy reform on its own, they gain when it is combined with the spread of the productivity-enhancing

FIGURE 3
Welfare Change from the Combination of Cotton Tariff and Subsidy Reform and Post-2001 GM Cotton Adoption, as a Per Cent of GDP, as a Multiple of the Percentage Change for the World as a Whole

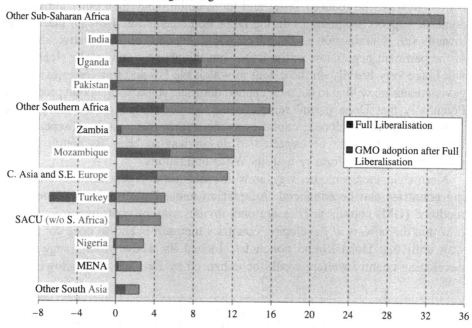

Source: Authors' GTAP model simulation results.

GM cotton varieties. Clearly this is an example of complementarity between the trade and development components of the Doha Cotton Initiative. In terms of sequencing, subsidy cuts first would expand the capacity of poor farmers in low-income countries to purchase the more-expensive GM cotton seeds and make the necessary adjustments to their farming practices, and thereby increase the prospects of realising the potential gains from GM adoption.

Finally, note that if Sub-Saharan Africa procrastinates on GM adoption while other developing countries embrace the new technology, net incomes of cotton farmers in the region are estimated to fall by seven per cent, whereas they rise by 10 per cent if Sub-Saharan Africa also adopts.[11] That difference of 17 percentage points is large even compared with the 31 per cent gain for the region's cotton farmers from full removal of all cotton subsidies and tariffs globally, but it is even larger when compared with the more likely gain of just eight per cent from the Doha partial reform simulation considered above.

7. CONCLUSIONS

The WTO's Hong Kong Trade Ministerial meeting of the Doha Development Agenda (DDA) in December 2005 agreed that cotton export subsidies be eliminated during 2006, that least-developed countries get duty-free access for their cotton exports by the time implementation of the DDA commences, and that domestic cotton subsidies be reduced faster and more ambitiously than other agricultural domestic support programmes during DDA implementation. How far that will go towards full liberalisation as examined above depends on the relative strengths of the pertinent negotiators in the DDA, but the above results make clear that it will hinge very heavily on the extent to which the US and to a lesser extent EU governments are willing to cut their applied domestic subsidies to cotton production. Potentially that Doha partial reform could deliver roughly twice the gains to cotton-exporting developing countries as the reform that – in the absence of the DDA – the US might be expected to do anyway to bring its cotton support programmes into conformity with its WTO obligations.

Meanwhile, there are other ways in which incomes of cotton farmers in developing countries can be enhanced. Adaptation and adoption of new genetically modified (GM) cotton varieties are one obvious way of contributing – and that is within the powers of developing countries themselves and so does not need to wait until that Doha Round concludes. Indeed the above results suggest that developing country welfare would be enhanced by far more from allowing GM

---

[11] As well, the health of GM cotton farmers improves, and there is less contamination of water and soil, following the switch to the less chemically-intensive Bt varieties of GM cotton. These extra benefits are not included in the above welfare calculus.

cotton adoption than by the removal of all cotton subsidies and tariffs.[12] Furthermore, our results support the notion that the gains to individual developing countries from reductions in trade-distorting cotton subsidies will be even greater if they allow GM cotton adoption first, providing yet another reason not to delay approval of this new biotechnology, especially since genetic modification of local cotton varieties and dissemination of the new technology to many small farmers will take some years. Perhaps some of the aid-for-trade funding that is being discussed as a complement to the DDA could facilitate that process.

REFERENCES

Alston, J. M., G. W. Edwards and J. W. Freebairn (1988), 'Market Distortions and Benefits from Research', *American Journal of Agricultural Economics*, **70**, 2, 281–88.

Anderson, K. and L. A. Jackson (2005), 'Some Implications of GM Food Technology Policies for Sub-Saharan Africa', *Journal of African Economies*, **14**, 3, 385–410.

Anderson, K. and W. Martin (eds.) (2006), *Agricultural Trade Reform and the Doha Development Agenda* (London: Palgrave Macmillan and Washington, DC: World Bank).

Anderson, K. and C. P. Nielsen (2004), 'Economic Effects of Agricultural Biotechnology Research in the Presence of Price-distorting Policies', *Journal of Economic Integration*, **19**, 2, 374–94.

Anderson, K. and E. Valenzuela (2006), 'The World Trade Organization's Doha Cotton Initiative: A Tale of Two Issues', CEPR Discussion Paper No. 5567 (London, March) and World Bank Policy Research Working Paper No. 3918 (May, Washington, DC).

Anderson, K., L. A. Jackson and C. P. Nielsen (2005), 'GM Rice Adoption: Implications for Welfare and Poverty Alleviation', *Journal of Economic Integration*, **20**, 4, 771–88.

Anderson, K., W. Martin and D. van der Mensbrugghe (2006), 'Would Multilateral Trade Reform Benefit Sub-Saharan Africa?', *Journal of African Economies*, **15**, 1, 626–70.

Anderson, K., W. Martin and E. Valenzuela (2006), 'The Relative Importance of Global Agricultural Subsidies and Market Access', *World Trade Review*, **5**, 3, 357–76.

Anderson, K., E. Valenzuela and L. A. Jackson (2008), 'Recent and Prospective Adoption of Genetically Modified Cotton: A Global CGE of Economic Impacts', *Economic Development and Cultural Change*, **56**, 2 (forthcoming).

Baffes, J. (2005), 'The "Cotton Problem"', *World Bank Research Observer*, **20**, 1, 109–43.

Dimaranan, B. V. (ed.) (2006), *Global Trade, Assistance, and Protection: The GTAP 6 Data Base* (Centre for Global Trade Analysis, Purdue University, West Lafayette).

FAO (2004), 'The Impact of Cotton Sector Support on Developing Countries: A Guide to Contemporary Analysis' (Mimeo, Food and Agriculture Organisation, Rome, September).

FAPRI (2005), *U.S. and World Agricultural Outlook 2005* (Ames, IA: Food and Agricultural Policy Institute, January, www.fapri.org).

Hertel, T. W. (ed.) (1997), *Global Trade Analysis: Modeling and Applications* (New York: Cambridge University Press).

Hossain, F., C. E. Pray, Y. Lu, J. Huang, C. Fan and R. Hu (2004), 'Genetically Modified Cotton and Farmers' Health in China', *International Journal of Occupational and Environmental Health*, **10**, 3, 296–303.

---

[12] If embracing GM cotton helped developing country governments to also streamline the process of approving the release of GM varieties of food crops, these economies would be able to multiply their estimated $2.3 billion gain from GM cotton adoption by at least two, according to the numbers presented in Anderson and Jackson (2005) and Anderson et al. (2005).

Huang, J., S. Rozelle and M. Chang (2004), 'The Nature of Distortions to Agricultural Incentives in China and Implications of WTO Accession', Ch. 6 in D. Bhattasali, S. Li and W. Martin (eds.), *China and the WTO* (London: Oxford University Press).

ICAC (2005), *The Outlook for Cotton Supply in 2005/06*, Secretariat of the International Cotton Advisory Committee (ICAC) (Washington, DC, September).

Marra, M., P. Pardey and J. Alston (2002), 'The Payoffs to Agricultural Biotechnology: An Assessment of the Evidence', *AgBioForum*, **5**, 2, 43–50 (Downloadable at http://www.agbioforum.org/v5n2/v5n2a02-marra.pdf).

OECD (2006), *Producer and Consumer Support Estimates, OECD Database 1986–2004* (at http://www.oecd.org/document/54/0,2340,en_2649_33727_35009718_1_1_1_1,00.html).

Qaim, M. and D. Zilberman (2003), 'Yield Effects of Genetically Modified Crops in Developing Countries', *Science*, **299**, 5608, 900–02.

Science Council (2005), *Science for Agricultural Development: Changing Concerns, New Opportunities* (Rome: Science Council of the CGIAR, December).

Shui, S. (2005), 'Policies Toward the Chinese Cotton Industry: The Commodity Chain Analysis Approach' (Mimeo, Commodities and Trade Division, FAO, Rome, February).

Sumner, D. A. (2005), 'Boxed in: Conflicts between U.S. Farm Policies and WTO Obligations', Trade Policy Analysis No. 32 (Cato Institute, Washington, DC, 5 December).

Sumner, D. A. (2006), 'Reducing Cotton Subsidies: The DDA Cotton Initiative', Ch. 10 in K. Anderson and W. Martin (eds.), *Agricultural Trade Reform and the Doha Development Agenda* (New York: Palgrave Macmillan and Washington, DC: World Bank).

van der Mensbrugghe, D. (2005), 'Linkage Technical Reference Document: Version 6.0' (The World Bank, Washington, DC, Mimeo, and at www.worldbank.org/prospects/linkagemodel).

WTO (2004a), *Decision Adopted by the General Council on 1 August 2004*, WT/L/579 (July Framework Agreement, (Geneva: World Trade Organisation, 2 August).

WTO (2004b), *United States – Subsidies on Upland Cotton: Report of the Panel*, WT/DS267/R (Geneva: World Trade Organisation, 8 September).

WTO (2004c), 'Agriculture: The Cotton Sub-Committee' (Geneva: World Trade Organisation, 19 November, at www.wto.org/english/tratop_e/agric_e/cotton_subcommittee_e.htm).

WTO (2005a), *United States – Subsidies on Upland Cotton: Report of the Appellate Body*, WT/DS267/AB/R (Geneva: World Trade Organisation, 3 March).

WTO (2005b), 'Ministerial Declaration: Doha Work Programme', WT/MIN(05)/DEC (Geneva: World Trade Organisation, 22 December, at www.wto.org/english/thewto_e/minist_e/min05_e/final_text_e.htm).

6

What is at Stake in the Doha Round?

Susanna Kinnman and Magnus Lodefalk

1. INTRODUCTION

IN 2001, the fourth ministerial meeting of the World Trade Organisation (WTO) was held in Doha, Qatar. This resulted in the launch of a new round of trade liberalisation negotiations, based on the so-called Doha Development Agenda (DDA), referring to the agreed central role of the development perspective in the negotiations. Since then several deadlines have passed without members reaching consensus in important areas. Negotiations still continue, but many view spring 2007 as the make-or-break moment for the Doha Round, in its current form.

What is at stake in the Doha negotiations? The aims of this study are to simulate and compare the effects of three potential Doha outcomes on national income and trade. Evidently, much remains to be agreed in the negotiations but already some features of a possible outcome can be discerned. Based on available information from the WTO negotiations, three illustrative scenarios are outlined, encompassing the areas of agriculture, non-agricultural market access (NAMA), services and trade facilitation. Trade facilitation has received special attention, in order to try to capture its appropriate contribution to overall gains. The scenarios are simulated using a quantitative framework, a so-called computable general equilibrium (CGE) model. These types of simulations are mainly useful in comparing medium-run effects and be the basis for discussions of relative changes in variables such as national income and trade. As any economic model, the one used in this study provides a simplified picture of the world economy and the results should be interpreted with great care. Furthermore, countries and sectors are aggregated into a smaller number of regions and sectors. This may affect simulation outcomes by underestimating global gains and concealing diverging results for individual countries or sectors within an aggregate group. Finally, dynamic

This paper is based upon a larger 2006 report *Economic Implications of the Doha Round* of the Board. For helpful comments and support, the authors are most grateful to Keith Walsh, Joe Francois, Håkan Nordström, other Board staff and a journal referee. For data assistance, they are indebted to Hanna Eriksson. Thanks also go to Peter Walkenhorst for sharing data on trade transaction costs. The usual caveat applies. Opinions expressed are solely the authors' own and do not necessarily reflect those of the Board or Sweden.

effects of trade liberalisation that are related to capital accumulation and general productivity growth are not incorporated into the main model. National income gains are therefore likely to be considerably underestimated.

The simulation results indicate that all groups of countries in this study benefit, with a particularly strong result for developing countries, including the LDCs. A conservative estimate is that real global income increases with 0.2–0.7 per cent of initial gross domestic product (GDP), depending on how far-reaching liberalisation takes place (when adding a dynamic link to the model, this figure rises).[1] Trade facilitation contributes the most to these national income results. This is not surprising considering that costs of delays in trade caused by cumbersome border procedure have been estimated at some 1–15 per cent of the value of world trade, and may be still higher for agro-food trade and for developing countries, including the LDCs.[2] To this can be added direct costs of border procedures, such as fees and formalities. In this study services liberalisation contributes the least to the global gains. This is partly attributed to the fact that only small real market openings are simulated, and that foreign direct investment (FDI) is not explicitly modelled.

Overall, simulations indicate the importance of countries' own liberalisation for their national income gains. Also, the results suggest that global income gains correspond to how far-reaching liberalisation takes place.

Compared to global gains estimated in other recent simulations, the results obtained in this study may seem somewhat low, 0.4 per cent of initial GDP in the core scenario (see Table 1). With the inclusion of the same liberalisation elements and using the same model, Francois et al. (2005) find global income gains of 0.5 per cent. However, this is mainly due to more moderate scenarios in this study. Compared to the simulation results in a paper by Anderson et al. (2006) the results in this study seem fairly reasonable, considering that they do not simulate liberalisation in the areas of services and trade facilitation.[3]

The outline of the paper is as follows. In Section 2, the method used and the design of the Doha scenarios are briefly explained. In Section 3, the global pre- and post-liberalisation environment is given. Section 4 presents the results on trade and national income. Finally, key findings are summarised and commented on in Section 5.[4]

---

[1] Henceforth, changes in national income are expressed in per cent of initial GDP, if not stated otherwise.

[2] OECD (2003).

[3] If including gains from these areas, results can be expected to be substantially higher. As shown in this and other studies, trade facilitation may contribute largely to global income gains, potentially as much as 40–50 per cent.

[4] More detailed information on the study design, data used, the robustness of the results and additional tables are available in the annexes to the full report, see the note at the bottom of the first page above.

TABLE 1

Estimates of Gains from Trade Liberalisation, in Per Cent of GDP and Billions of US Dollars

Study	Model	Liberalisation Elements				Global Gains	
		Agriculture	Manufactures	Services	Trade Facilitation	Doha Scenario	Full Liberalisation
This study	Standard*	X	X	X	X	0.3% ($80 bn)	1.2% ($369 bn)
	Imperfect competition**	X	X	X	X	**0.4% ($117 bn)**	**1.7% ($540 bn)**
Polaski (2006)	Standard but with technological change, sluggish real wages and two forms of unskilled labour	X	X			0.2% ($59 bn)	0.5% ($168 bn)
Anderson et al. (2006)	Model with dynamics, macroeconomic projections and high elasticities	X	X			0.2% ($96 bn)	0.7% ($287 bn)
Matthews and Walsh (2005)	Standard but with macroeconomic projections	X	X	X	X	0.3% ($120 bn)	
Francois et al. (2005)	Imperfect competition**	X	X	X	X	0.5% ($158 bn)	

Notes:
* Signifying a static CGE model with perfect competition and constant returns to scale.
** Static CGE model with monopolistic competition and increasing returns to scale.

2. METHOD AND SCENARIOS

The global system of international trade constitutes a complex web of inter-linkages in the form of flows of goods, capital and services. Through these linkages even moderate changes in a sector or country may have effects else-where. When several changes are implemented simultaneously – for example, in reforming the trade policy of a country – it can be even more difficult to foresee what the overall outcome will be on different sectors and countries. In order to capture these linkages, computable general equilibrium models (CGE models) are often used.[5]

In CGE models, sectors and countries are inter-linked and all markets are presumed to clear, i.e. demand equals supply, both initially and after markets have adjusted to the policy reforms, indicating a medium-run perspective. CGE models are useful to display *relative* changes in variables such as real national income, export, import, prices etc., at sector as well as at country level. The results are primarily useful to rank policies and to act as a basis for discussion of potential effects of trade liberalisation. National income gains are represented by the change in the real value of consumption and savings, considering income as well as price changes.[6] Several assumptions about actors' behaviour and the character or availability of goods and services are always present in CGE models. For example, the employment level of factors of production, such as labour, is commonly presumed to be constant, as in this study. This might underestimate national income gains for some countries and overestimate gains for others. The assumptions of the model will influence the simulation results and may constitute limitations.

In this study, a modified version of a standard CGE model – GTAP – has been used.[7] GTAP is a widely used comparative static model, with an associated database, that has been applied in several of the recent analyses of trade liberal-isation.[8] The standard GTAP model, which assumes perfect competition and constant returns to scale, has in this study been modified to incorporate scale economies and imperfect competition in some of the sectors,[9] along the lines of Francois et al. (2005).[10] This is due to trade not only being generated by the

---

[5] For an introduction to these types of economic models and their limitations, see e.g., Piermartini and Teh (2005).

[6] Income changes include changes in factor returns as well as in net government transfers. Technically, national income gains are changes in economic welfare, which in turn is measured as equivalent variation (EV).

[7] Global Trade Analysis Project, Hertel (1997).

[8] The model and database have recently been used in, e.g., Matthews and Walsh (2005) and Francois et al. (2005), and the database in, e.g., Anderson et al. (2006).

[9] In manufactures and processed food sectors. There are arguments for using the same specification for some of the services sectors but this has not been done, mainly because of a lack of data.

[10] A monopolistic competition specification that implies liberalisation effects from changes in the number of available product varieties. In effect, this mimics (external) scale economy effects.

traditional neoclassical argument of comparative advantage,[11] but also by economies of scale and a demand for more diversified goods ('love of variety'). Results of this main model are compared with results of the standard GTAP model as well as a modified version of the main model that also captures dynamics between changes in income, savings and capital accumulation.[12]

The latest version of the GTAP database, version 6, provides a snapshot of world trade, production and relevant policies in 2001. To facilitate the analysis, we have aggregated countries and industries into 16 regions and 21 sectors. The database has been updated in a pre-experiment to account for some important economic policy changes preceding full implementation of the Doha Round outcome, here interpreted as 2015. Only those economic changes that have been judged most relevant for this specific study have been included, namely: implementation of previously agreed WTO commitments; China's accession to the WTO; addition of new members to the EU; reforms of the EU's agricultural policy; and implementation of the EU's Everything But Arms Initiative (EBA). The updated database constitutes the reference scenario; that is, the baseline with which results from the simulations of the Doha scenarios will be compared.[13]

Three reform scenarios have been outlined for this study. Although carefully crafted, the scenarios are illustrative rather than descriptive and draw upon available negotiation information up to the WTO Geneva meeting in July 2006. The main difference between the three is the extent of liberalisation in the different areas. The core scenario constitutes middle ground, and will be compared with results from less and more far-reaching liberalisation scenarios. In all three scenarios, elements included are: tariff reductions; removal of agricultural export subsidies; lowering of agricultural domestic support; increased services market access; and trade facilitation. Apart from trade facilitation, the least developed countries (LDCs) are in this study not expected to undertake any commitments in the round.[14] Other elements, such as commitments on non-tariff barriers to trade and rules reform, are not considered. Finally, a full liberalisation scenario, encompassing the same negotiation areas, is simulated for reference purpose.

To illustrate the level of liberalisation in the scenarios it can be noted that in the core scenario, the average *applied* tariff is reduced with 16 per cent for manufactures and 23 per cent for agricultural goods, globally.[15] For services, the core scenario implies that global costs related to services market barriers are

---

[11] The two main sources of comparative advantage are differences in the global distribution of factors of production and differences in production technologies of countries.

[12] This dynamic model version does not incorporate general productivity growth. Although adding dynamics means capturing more of the expected gains from liberalisation, it involves further assumptions. The model is therefore mainly used for comparison.

[13] Other changes such as population growth and technological change are not considered, for simplicity.

[14] With the exception of a commitment to bind tariffs.

[15] Simple averages across countries.

reduced with approximately 0.7 per cent of the value of the imported service, on average. Regarding trade facilitation, costs arising from export and import waiting times and from border fees, formalities etc. are reduced. Taking Brazil as an example, the average waiting time in Brazil is simulated to be reduced with some 1–5 days, for manufactures,[16] depending on how far-reaching facilitation efforts are made. The cost savings of these efforts in Brazil are simulated to be 0.5–2.6 per cent of the value of the traded goods, for manufactures.[17] In the core scenario, it is assumed that global trade costs arising from border delays are reduced with 0.7 per cent of the value of the traded goods, on average. At the same time direct costs are reduced, resulting in a further average cut of 1.05 per cent in global trade costs.

In the scenarios, all reductions of tariffs and agricultural domestic support are estimated on the level of the study's sectors, and performed in two steps. First, the new bound rates of each sector are estimated by applying the reduction formulas to the bound base rates.[18] Second, real reductions are simulated in the model, but only to the extent that the new bound levels are lower than the actually applied ones.[19] This two-step procedure is used in order to avoid overestimating liberalisation efforts, since it is a relatively frequent practice to have a significant gap between the bound and applied tariff rates – a so-called 'binding overhang'.

In the area of non-agricultural market access (NAMA), tariffs are cut using a so-called Swiss tariff reduction formula.[20] The formula is harmonising, which means that higher tariff rates are reduced the most. In this study, two different coefficients are used for industrial and developing countries, excluding the LDCs, whereby industrial countries liberalise the most.[21] In addition, very low tariffs ('nuisance tariffs') in industrial countries are removed in the scenario with more far-reaching liberalisation.[22] It has been estimated that the EU's average *bound* tariff on manufactures is 2.9 per cent before the liberalisation. The reduction formula and rates used in this study's core scenario have been estimated to imply a decrease of the EU's average bound rate with approximately 59 per cent.[23]

---

[16] From an initial waiting time of 12.4 days.

[17] To this should be added cost-savings from shorter export waiting times elsewhere and from reductions in fees and formalities when imported.

[18] Members' tariff rates are bound in the WTO, i.e. they constitute the maximum rates that a member may apply. Data on bound rates were withdrawn from COMTRADE and TRAINS database, using the integrated system WITS. In WITS trade-weighted estimates for the GTAP sectors' tariffs can be found, as well as *ad valorem* equivalents.

[19] Applied rates in year 2001 are used in the GTAP database.

[20] At the Hong Kong ministerial (WTO, 2005) members agreed to use a Swiss formula. Here a simple Swiss formula is used: $T1 = (T0 * a)/(T0 + a)$; with new tariff ($T1$), current tariff ($T0$), and coefficient (a).

[21] Coefficients used for industrial countries in the three scenarios are 5, 10 and 15 in the scenarios with more liberalisation, the core scenario and the one with less liberalisation, and for developing countries the corresponding numbers are 15, 20 and 30.

[22] Here defined as tariffs equal to or lower than three per cent.

[23] Own calculations, weighted on global import (1999–2001) and using countries' own estimates of base tariffs submitted to the WTO.

Agricultural liberalisation includes tariff cuts, by using a linear and harmonising approach.[24] The reduction rates of the core scenario have previously been
estimated to lead to a reduction of the average agricultural *bound* tariff in the EU
by 55 per cent.[25] For developing countries, the percentage cuts in bound tariffs are
two-thirds of the tariff cuts of industrial countries. In the scenario with more far-
reaching liberalisation, so-called 'caps' on tariffs will be implemented. This implies
that no tariff rates are allowed above a maximum limit. Exemptions from tariff
reductions for so-called sensitive and special products are not included in any
scenario.[26] Another element of agricultural liberalisation is reductions in domestic
support. Because of difficulties in representing reductions in domestic support,
only the most trade-distorting form of support, the so-called amber support, will
be reduced.[27] Countries with the highest total bound support levels are assumed
to make the largest reductions.[28] As there is a substantial gap between bound and
applied levels for most regions this only results in real cuts in some regions and
sectors.[29] The final element of agricultural liberalisation that will be simulated in
this study is the complete removal of agricultural export subsidies.

The simulation of services trade liberalisation is highly stylised and involves
cutting tariff equivalents of estimated barriers to trade in different sectors and
regions. The reductions take the form of partial convergence to 'best practice'.[30]
It can be assumed that most commitments under the Doha Round will just involve
binding existing practice and that new real market opportunities will therefore be

---

[24] The tariffs are put into four intervals according to how high they are. For the industrial countries
the following intervals and reduction rates (in per cent) are used in the core scenario: 0–30, 31–60,
61–90, >90 intervals, and 43, 53, 58, 68 per cent cuts. Intervals for the developing countries:
0–30, 31–80, 81–130, >130, and 30, 37, 40 and 47 per cent cuts. The scenario is based on an EU
offer (EU, 2005) plus an additional eight percentage unit cut added in each band.

[25] Swedish Board of Agriculture (2006) calculations. In these estimates an agricultural tariff cap
of 100 per cent is assumed, thereby differing from this study's core scenario. For comparison, the G20
(2005) proposal is said to result in 54 and 36 per cent average cuts for industrial and developing
countries.

[26] Not taking these exemptions into account can be expected to overestimate the global gains from
liberalisation. On the other hand, the sectoral aggregation of the study is likely to lead to under-
estimation of potential gains, and this particularly applies to agriculture.

[27] Reductions are made to direct support to production ('to' in GTAP notation) and direct support
to inputs used in production ('tfd' and 'tfm' in GTAP notation). Reductions in market price support
(mps) is not modelled.

[28] Countries are put in three different bands according to the level of the total bound domestic
support: EU will have to make the largest reductions (in the core scenario: 90 per cent), US and
Japan (80 per cent), and all other industrialised regions (70 per cent). Developing countries are
assumed to make reductions by two-thirds the rate of industrialised countries.

[29] In the core scenario only Switzerland, Rep. of Korea and Norway are assumed to be affected by
the reductions, with −21, −34 and −43 per cent respectively.

[30] Best practice in a specific sector is the lowest tariff equivalent of all regions in our aggregation.
Convergence ratios in less, core and more scenarios are: 5, 10 and 20 per cent. Tariff equivalents
are estimated mainly by drawing upon data by Kalirajan (2000), McGuire et al. (2000); McGuire
and Schuele (2000); Nguyen-Hong (2000); and Warren (2000).

limited. The reduction rates that we use are rather modest and the convergence ratio is the same for all countries and sectors. The average cost reduction for the global services sector is approximately 0.7 per cent of the value of services import.

In the highly stylised trade facilitation scenarios, all countries undertake commitments but their absolute commitments differ, as it is related to how far from best practice they are.[31] The scenarios imply that improvements in border procedures are modelled in most countries. This seems realistic considering progress in this area of the Doha negotiations. Still, to a large extent, these trade facilitation efforts hinge on fulfilment of expected commitments by industrial countries to provide necessary financial and technical support to the LDCs and to other developing countries.[32] As for services liberalisation, reduction in the tariff equivalents of border procedures is simulated by a (partial) convergence to best practice. Tariff equivalents are estimated for indirect as well as for direct costs of border procedures (trade transaction costs, TTCs), such as costs for border delays and for fees and documentation costs respectively. As a result of removing direct TTCs governments will, at least initially, lose revenue from fees and charges, and employees engaged in border procedures will have to move to other employment. These adjustment costs are considered in the model, while implementation costs for the reforms are not. Tariff equivalents of border procedures are modelled to be higher for countries not belonging to the OECD and for agricultural products.[33] Moreover, trade facilitation efforts are in this study presumed to reduce costs for exports as well as imports, but there is somewhat more an emphasis on the potential for cost-savings on the import side.

3. THE WORLD ECONOMY PRE- AND POST-LIBERALISATION

In order to get a better understanding of the changes taking place after trade liberalisation, it can be useful to look at the economic structures and policy environment, before and after the reform. To get a schematic overview, the world economy is divided into four country groups – the EU27,[34] other industrial countries (OICs), the LDCs and other developing countries (ODCs) – and three aggregate sectors – agricultural goods, manufactures and services.

---

[31] Best practice is the lowest tariff equivalent of all regions' estimates in the aggregation, and the convergence ratios are 10, 20 and 50 per cent in the less, core and more scenarios. Estimates are mainly based upon data by World Bank (2005) whereas the methodology draws heavily on OECD (2003).

[32] It can be added that, with respect to trade facilitation, there are a number of reforms that are relatively cheap, easy to implement and that can constitute the first basic steps in improving border procedures (Swedish National Board of Trade, 2003). Two examples of such reform are to limit requirements for duplicate information and to apply new laws only after their publication.

[33] Compared with tariff equivalents for OECD countries and for manufactures, respectively.

[34] The present 25 member states plus Romania and Bulgaria.

The first sub-section gives an overview of the reference scenario – the baseline – to which the outcome of the simulated Doha Round will be compared. In the second sub-section the simulation results from the core Doha scenario, as described in the introductory chapter, are used for the representation of the post-Doha situation. Data accounted for is based on own calculations on data deriving from the GTAP database, if not mentioned otherwise.

a. The Pre-liberalisation Economy

(i) The pre-liberalisation trade and production structures

In the reference scenario EU27, other industrial countries and the developing countries have approximately the same sectoral trade structures. Manufactures represent the largest share of world trade (approximately 70 per cent of total import), followed by services (around 20 per cent), and finally agricultural goods (6–8 per cent).[35] For the LDC group, the size order of the different import sectors is the same, but the distribution between the three sectors is more even: 50, 33 and 17 per cent.

The most important share in global production is the services sector, representing 62 per cent of total global production. For the group of other industrial countries, it represents more than two-thirds of the total value of production. The share of agriculture seems to have an inverted relationship to the level of development, as it is largest in LDCs, and decrease in importance as the level of development increases.

(ii) The pre-liberalisation policy environment

The policy environment for manufactures and agricultural goods prior to liberalisation is shown in Table 2. The figures represent *applied ad valorem* tariff rates, which have been estimated by taking the total value, *including* taxes/subsidies, divided by the value *excluding* taxes/subsidies. The estimates also include the direct costs for trade procedures that have been added in the database as additional border taxes.[36]

In the initial data, industrial countries' tariffs on manufactures are comparatively low, on average around four to five per cent (Table 2). However, this figure does not tell the whole story, as almost 10 per cent of industrial countries' tariff rates are substantially higher (Fernandez de Córdoba et al., 2004, p. 5), so-called tariff peaks. Developing countries in general have higher bound tariffs on manufactures,

---

[35] On the export side, the sector's shares in total value mirrors to a large extent the import side.

[36] These rates may differ greatly from the rates bound in the WTO, because of 'binding overhangs'. Also, the average weighted tariff rates are contingent on the sources of a country's import as well as the mix of the import products. Thus, a region's applied weighted tariff rate may decrease even without a policy change if its import patterns change. This way of estimating distortions can also conceal substantial taxes and subsidies as these are evened out on the net level.

TABLE 2
Net Tariffs and Subsidies, Pre-Doha
(In per cent of value)

Policy Instruments	EU27	OIC	LDC	ODC	Global Average
Import Tariffs (tms)					
Agricultural goods	15.8	19.2	28.2	26.5	21.7
Manufactures	4.4	4.7	78.7	12.1	7.9
Agricultural Export Subsidies (txs)					
(neg. value = nettax)	3.4	−3.5	−3.5	−3.6	−2.5
Agricultural Domestic Support					
Output subsidies (to)* (neg. value = net tax)	−1.0	−1.8	−2.1	−1.8	−1.7
Intermediate input subsidies on domestic goods (tfd) (neg. value = net subsidy)	0.8	−0.7	0.0	0.1	−0.0
Intermediate input subsidies on imported goods (tfm) (neg. value = net subsidy)	0.8	−0.5	0.1	0.0	0.2
Effective Tariff Equivalents**					
Services	4.0	4.9	11.4	14.5	7.4

Notes:
* Data indicate that there is a net tax on the overall production in the agricultural sector. ** The estimated tariff equivalent in a region minus the one in the region which represents 'best practice'. The estimate is not to be confused with the actual service barrier, but interpreted as the difference between a country's barriers and the barriers of the country with best practice.

Source: Own calculations based on GTAP-simulation results.

but there is often a significant gap between bound and applied most-favoured-nation (MFN) tariff rates – a so-called 'binding overhang'.[37] In addition, developing countries still have comparatively low binding coverage. When looking at the average *applied* tariff rate for other developing countries', as seen in Table 2, it is higher than for industrial countries. The group of LDCs has by far the highest average tariff (almost 80 per cent). Again, it should be noted that this figure includes direct costs related to cumbersome border procedures. Finally, it can be noted that the difference between the tariffs of industrial and developing countries is much larger for manufactures than for agricultural goods. One reason for this difference is that industrial countries to a larger extent have participated fully in extensive multilateral industrial liberalisation efforts since the creation of the GATT (the precursor of the WTO). Another reason is that many industrial countries have pursued sectoral liberalisation of manufactures in the WTO, resulting in low or zero tariffs for substantial parts of their tariffs for manufactures.

---

[37] For example, the average G20 bound tariff is 30 per cent, while the applied MFN duty is 13 per cent (WTO, 2002). The MFN rule is a core WTO principle that *inter alia* means that a tariff concession to one member automatically has to be extended to all others and the new rate constitutes the MFN duty.

Unlike the tariffs for manufactures, most WTO members, including the developing countries, have bound their agricultural tariffs within the WTO. The global average for bound agricultural tariffs has been estimated to 62 per cent, with large variation between countries and products (Gibson et al., 2001). As seen in Table 2, the applied tariffs are much lower, indicating the existence of high binding overhang. Also, because of the existence of high and sometimes prohibitive tariffs for some agricultural goods – leading to no or only very limited trade – a non-trade-weighted average would be considerably higher. According to the data, the group of LDCs has the highest average agricultural tariff, followed by the other developing countries.

Among the country groups in Table 2, net agricultural export subsidies are only observed for agricultural goods exported from the EU.[38] As to domestic support, all regions have a net tax on this aggregate level, and only the estimate for the group of other industrial countries shows positive production subsidies; this even though 25 countries/regions (EU27 counted as one) have bound their levels of such support in the WTO. When looking at a more detailed level it can be noted that this is mainly due to taxes in the processed food and beverages sector (processed food sector).

Restrictions on trade in services add an extra cost on the imports of services, which can be estimated as a tariff equivalent. In turn, the term 'effective' tariff equivalents will in this study be used to indicate the protection above best practice. The averages of the effective tariff equivalents used in this study are shown in Table 2. The EU and the other industrial countries (OIC) have the lowest barriers to trade in services, followed by developing countries (ODCs), and finally the LDCs. These data should be treated with caution, as they are only rough estimates deriving from the scarce data that exist on the subject,[39] which have further been adjusted to fit for this specific study. Moreover, since the estimates derive from studies of different services sectors in the late 1990s, they do not account for the changes that have taken place since.[40]

b. The Post-liberalisation Economy

The simulation results from the core Doha scenario are used for the representation of the post-liberalisation situation.

---

[38] In all other regions, except agricultural exports of LDCs, the figures indicate an export tax, at this aggregate level, but the figures may hide substantial export subsidies for specific products. The rates also include the estimated direct costs for cumbersome border procedures.

[39] For data used, see the technical annex to the full report referred to in the note at the bottom of the first page above.

[40] For example, in the 1990s the telecommunications sector was highly regulated in several countries. Since then many countries have opened up for competition in this sector. This implies that the benchmark levels used may be substantially overestimated. However, since the reductions are modelled as convergence towards best practice, the actual level is less relevant for the results.

(i) Trade structures after liberalisation

When comparing the trade structure in the simulated post-Doha scenario with the baseline, some changes can be observed. Trade in services has become a smaller part of total trade for all country groups, whereas share of trade in merchandise has increased. This reflects the assumption in this study that real liberalisation efforts are primarily made in manufactures and agriculture, rather than in services, resulting in different impacts on shares of overall trade. Globally, the largest import rise takes place in the share of agriculture imports of the group of other industrial countries', followed by the group of LDCs. For the EU the agriculture export share and the manufacture import share have both declined, though the latter only marginally.

The largest export change takes place in the shares of agricultural export of other developing countries (ODCs) which increases with 17 per cent, at the cost of services which decreases with about 13 per cent. The production structures in industrial and developing countries are almost unchanged, after the simulated Doha Round. In most country groups there are mainly small changes in the production shares of agriculture and manufactures. In the EU, the share of agriculture in overall production has decreased with almost five per cent, while it has increased with almost three per cent in developing countries (ODCs). In the two developing groups, the share of manufactures has declined with two to three per cent.

(ii) The post-Doha policy environment

In the post-Doha scenario, import tariffs have been considerably reduced, in regions that are simulated to undertake commitments in this area. In particular, this applies to tariffs on agricultural goods entering the EU. Globally, the average applied tariffs are cut the most for manufactures, by 22 per cent. However, it should be added that the reduction rates also include cuts in the direct costs, associated with cumbersome border procedures (trade facilitation). Agricultural export subsidies have been removed in countries with commitments in the area.[41] Regarding the reductions in the domestic support rates, only minor changes can be observed. This is due to the large gap between bound and applied support rates. For services imports, effective tariff equivalents are reduced by 10 per cent across regions, as specified in the core scenario.

4. THE GLOBAL ECONOMIC IMPLICATIONS OF THE ROUND

In this section, results from the simulations of the Doha scenarios are presented and analysed, starting with changes to trade and production patterns and continuing with effects on national income. If not otherwise indicated, the results

---

[41] This has mainly affected the EU which had an initially high net subsidy.

TABLE 3
Exports by Source and Destination (Per cent change, value f.o.b.) – Core Scenario

↓ From → To	EU27	OIC	LDC	ODC	Total Exports
EU27	−3	5	1	14	2
OIC	6	6	6	15	9
LDC	1	14	16	10	8
ODC	13	12	11	16	14
Total Imports	*2*	*8*	*7*	*15*	*7*

Source: GTAP model simulation results.

are based on simulations with the *main model*, i.e. the model with imperfect competition and increasing returns to scale.

Multilateral trade liberalisation can be expected to create trade as well as change trade patterns. Starting with the trade-creating effect, the simulation results indicate an increase in global exports with seven per cent in the core scenario (Table 3). Results of the scenario with more far-reaching liberalisation show an increase in trade value with 16 per cent, while the export growth is four per cent in the scenario with a lower level of liberalisation. Turning to effects on trade patterns, the change in trade flows between the different groups can be observed in Table 3.

Looking at the top row of the first column, the results indicate a decline in the intra-EU trade with some three per cent. This is explained by the eroding 'preferences' for intra-EU goods and services when tariffs on imports from non-EU regions are reduced. However, exports to other industrial countries and especially other developing countries (ODCs) increase. As EU trade is dominated by trade within the Union, the increase only results in a slightly higher overall export figure, when the Doha commitments are implemented. This result is maintained even in the scenario with more far-reaching liberalisation. Looking at the second row of Table 3, the change in export value for other industrial countries is positive to all regions, but here also especially to the group of developing countries (ODCs).

The trade of developing countries, including the LDCs, grows more than the trade of industrial countries, and their share of world trade increases as more far-reaching liberalisation takes place. In particular, overall trade between developing countries grows considerably. This is the effect of liberalisation of trade in merchandise and services as well as of trade facilitation.[42]

As for the LDCs, their export to the EU27 increases only marginally. Prior to the simulated liberalisation, LDCs had preferential access to the EU market, through

---

[42] The increase in overall trade between developing countries should not be sensitive to exceptions from liberalisation in a single issue area.

TABLE 4
National Income Effects for Country Groups
(Billion USD and per cent of initial GDP)

	Less		Core		More		Full	
	Bn USD	Per Cent	Bn USD	Per Cent	Bn USD	Per Cent	Bn USD	Per Cent
EU27	16	0.2	23	0.3	29	0.4	65	0.8
OIC	23	0.1	37	0.2	65	0.4	171	1.0
LDC	3	0.7	5	1.3	12	3.0	36	9.0
ODC	29	0.5	51	0.8	124	2.0	267	4.4
GLOBAL	71	0.2	117	0.4	229	0.7	540	1.7

Source: GTAP-simulation results.

the EBA and the Cotonou agreement. This preference is eroded when import barriers for goods and services from other regions are reduced in the simulations.

The main simulation effect of the Doha Round on regions' integration in the global economy is the opening up of developing countries, excluding the LDCs, changing from a trade/GDP ratio of 60 per cent to 68 per cent. This can be compared with the effect globally, where the ratio increases from 44 to 47 per cent.

So far focus has been on the implications of the simulations on trade and production patterns. These changes can be expected to affect national income.[43] In Table 4 the simulation effects on real national income from the different Doha scenarios are given.

The results from a simulation of the core Doha scenario show an increase in global income by 0.4 per cent. This is equivalent to 117 billion US dollars (in 2001 dollars).[44] Simulations of the scenario with less far-reaching liberalisation indicate that gains are reduced to 65 per cent of the core scenario (0.2 per cent of GDP), whereas with more liberalisation the gains from the core scenario double (0.7 per cent of GDP). In other words, income gains roughly correspond to liberalisation efforts. For reference, these results can be compared with the gains from a full liberalisation scenario, where global income increases with 1.7 per cent (or 540 bn USD). In all three main scenarios, the LDCs benefit the most in relation to initial GDP, followed by other developing countries and finally the industrial countries, including the EU. When more far-reaching liberalisation takes place – including larger commitments for developing countries, including the LDCs – developing countries' part in the global gains increases to 60 per cent of global gains.

[43] Technically, 'national income' stands for economic welfare gains, measured as equivalent variation (EV). EV is a measure of how much more money (in 2001 years mn USD) a consumer would need, in the pre-liberalisation situation to be as well off as in the post-liberalisation situation.
[44] In this report, real national income changes are either expressed as percentage changes in initial GDP, or in 2001 dollars. It can be added that global gains roughly triple when comparing gains in the main model with those of a model with dynamics from capital accumulation.

The largest share of the global economic gains can be derived from more efficient allocation of resources, i.e. resources are moved to sectors where they are more productive. This effect accounts for 39 per cent of the total global gains in the core scenario and is one of the main contributors to gains for most countries of the study and especially for developing countries. Of these gains, the textiles, clothing and footwear sector ('textiles') represents almost 25 per cent, in the core scenario.

The second largest contributor to global income changes, and indeed the key source of gains for industrialised countries, is the scale economies effect (32 per cent, in the core scenario). This effect is the result of the modelling of monopolistic competition in some sectors.[45] The outcome is comparable with the effect from better exploitation of (external) economies of scale. For the EU, this effect becomes increasingly important as more liberalisation takes place.

The contribution of the scale economies effect in the overall national income gains is related to which sectors are expanding: if the expansion takes place in sectors modelled with no (or low) economies of scale at the cost of production in sectors with economies of scale, the effect will be negative. This can be observed in the case of India, as the expansion of services has a negative impact on the overall income gains.[46] Similarly, China's significant specialisation in textiles has the negative effect of drawing resources from other manufactures sectors, most of which have higher mark-ups.[47] In contrast, South African expansion in the other manufactures sector contributes to income gains, as the sector is modelled to exhibit important economies of scale. Still, it should be recognised that although sectoral expansion certainly matters for national income it does not alter the qualitative overall outcome for any country in the study.

Another important source of national income gains is an increased efficiency in the import of goods and services, as a consequence of reducing indirect trade barriers. The liberalisation of trade procedures and services regulations makes imports available to consumers and producers at lower prices, leading to national income gains. This effect represents approximately 30 per cent of the global gains in the core scenario but takes on in importance with more liberalisation.

The fourth factor that may influence the income effects from liberalisation is the terms-of-trade effect. A positive terms-of-trade effect implies that prices of a region's export increases in relation to the prices of that region's import. Although per definition zero at the global level, for some regions the effect is important. When simulating the effects of the core Doha scenario, industrialised

---

[45] The specification is based on the assumption that consumers benefit from more product varieties whereas producers benefit from more varieties in intermediate goods.

[46] However, there are arguments for also modelling some services sectors with economies of scale. As mentioned in the text, this has not been done mainly because of a lack of data.

[47] Mark-up (price over marginal cost) is an indication of market concentration.

TABLE 5
National Income Effects – Whose Liberalisation Benefits Whom
(Per cent of total global gains), Core Scenario

Liberalising Region Benefiting Region	Agriculture	Manufactures	Services	Trade Facilitation	Total
IC					
IC	8.9	12.2	2.1	8.6	31.8
DC	−0.5	4.9	0.0	9.2	13.6
Total	*8.4*	*17.1*	*2.0*	*17.8*	*45.4*
DC					
IC	1.5	12.1	−0.1	6.4	19.8
DC	5.6	4.5	2.8	21.8	34.8
Total	*7.1*	*16.6*	*2.7*	*28.3*	*54.6*
All					
IC	10.4	24.3	1.9	15.0	51.6
DC	5.2	9.4	2.8	31.0	48.4
Total	*15.5*	*33.7*	*4.7*	*46.0*	*100.0*

Source: GTAP-simulation results.

countries, and the EU in particular, experience negative terms-of-trade effects, while changes in the terms of trade favour developing countries.[48]

Looking at the geographical sources of the national income effects, i.e. whose liberalisation benefits whom it can be observed that the largest gains for developing countries, including the LDCs, derive from own liberalisation. Indeed, for most countries domestic liberalisation contributes substantially to a country's gain from the Round.[49]

Divided into the different negotiation areas, results from the simulation of the core Doha scenario indicate that almost half of the economic gains, 46 per cent, derives from trade facilitation (Table 5). Especially reforms in developing countries (including the LDCs) contribute to these gains, and developing countries gain the most from reforms in this area. The role of trade facilitation for global gains is not surprising considering the substantial costs related to cumbersome border procedure that have been estimated by, for example, the OECD (2003).

---

[48] With more liberalisation, these effects are even more pronounced for the EU and developing countries.
[49] The sequencing of reforms may affect simulation gains attributed to each reform. In this paper this is considered by using the decomposition algorithm of Harrison et al. (2000), which is included in the GEMPACK software accompanying GTAP version 6. However, the reduction of direct trade transaction costs (TTCs) have been performed in two steps, something which may affect results because of potential path dependency. Still, changing the sequencing does neither affect the overall result nor the regional gains significantly. The major gains from trade facilitation come from reducing indirect rather than direct TTCs. (In the simulations, direct TTC cuts contribute with some 10 per cent of the global gains of the round.)

The second most important source for national income gains is increased market access for manufactures, representing about a third of all the gains from the simulation.

Gains from agricultural liberalisation come in third place (16 per cent), with the major share coming from improved market access. Somewhat unexpected, the results indicate that the agricultural liberalisation of industrial countries that is simulated has a negligible effect on national income in developing countries. These results may seem surprising considering agriculture's central role in the negotiations. However, this is on an aggregate level. When looking at a more detailed level, the individual regions or countries show diverging results, as some win and others lose from industrial countries' liberalisation. The outcome for an individual country will to a large extent depend on if a country benefits or loses from changes in prices on agricultural products (net-importer or net-exporter). Also, for developing countries as a group, the share of agriculture in trade in goods has decreased dramatically over the last three decades. Industrial countries' reductions in domestic and export subsidies is generally benefiting themselves rather than developing countries, as this allows resources in industrial countries to be used more efficiently.[50] Nevertheless, considering the importance of the agricultural sector for many developing countries and for development and poverty alleviation, these results underline the need for more far-reaching agricultural commitments than in the two scenarios with lower levels of liberalisation. This is necessary in order to realise the potential of agricultural liberalisation to contribute significantly to the gains of developing countries.[51]

Finally, the liberalisation of services only corresponds to five per cent of the global income gains. This is lower than in most other studies. Besides the fact that rather modest reduction rates are used in this study (because of the high expected rate of 'binding overhang'), this is most likely a consequence of letting the barriers converge towards a benchmark, instead of using zero as an estimate for a liberalised market. Moreover, since most of the services are produced and consumed in the same country, cross-border trade in services only accounts for approximately a quarter of the total trade.[52]

---

[50] The aggregation of many sectors into only a few agricultural sectors is also likely to dampen the overall results from agricultural liberalisation. On the other hand, the omission of so-called flexibilities where tariffs on some products are not reduced is likely to overestimate gains from increased agricultural market access.

[51] The agricultural sector employs over 60 per cent of the population in developing countries, and over 70 per cent in LDCs. It is also estimated that 70 per cent of the world's poorest people live in rural areas, which makes it central for the alleviation of poverty.

[52] Only one of the four modes of supply within the area of services liberalisation is explicitly modelled in the GTAP model (cross-border supply). Taking into account the value shares of these modes in total services trade, therefore, only approximately a third of the value of the services trade is liberalised in the simulations.

The size order of the negotiation areas' contribution to national income remains the same with more far-reaching liberalisation. However, with a lower level of liberalisation, market access for manufactures replaces trade facilitation as the key contributor to global gains. The share of trade facilitation gains increase with more liberalisation, and the contribution of such reforms to developing countries in particular. Still, to realise these gains from trade facilitation developing countries, and especially the LDCs, will need substantial support in reforming their border procedures.

5. CONCLUSIONS AND FINAL COMMENTS

In this study the effects of potential outcomes of the WTO Doha trade negotiations on national income and trade have been analysed. The analysis has been performed by applying a computable simulation model of the world economy (GTAP) that is commonly used internationally. Three stylised scenarios have been simulated. The main difference between the scenarios is the extent of liberalisation. In several areas, it seems as if the core scenario of this study could be rather close to potential landing zones of the negotiations.

A great deal is at stake in the Doha Round. The simulations of the stylised Doha scenarios indicate potential global income gains of 0.2–0.7 per cent (71–230 bn USD), depending on the level of trade liberalisation.[53] (With dynamics from capital accumulation results are magnified substantially, 0.7–2.5 per cent (or 220–770 bn USD).[54]) These results may seem somewhat low when compared with the results of similar studies, but they can mainly be explained by more moderate scenarios than in other previous work.

The results from the model simulations indicate that all regional groups in the study would gain from implementing the Doha scenarios if national income effects are looked at. However, if some elements of the Doha agenda are excluded from the simulations, a few turn out to be losers. This indicates that a broad-based round is key to boost global and national income while avoiding or at the least minimising the risk of some countries turning out to be net losers. Finally, it should be noted that even with a broad-based round, if all countries were separate entities in the simulations, some of the less developed countries may not have the capacity to adjust to the new trade opportunities. Therefore, to ensure that every WTO member can take advantage of new market openings and become a net-winner from liberalisation, adjustment assistance as well as compensation for eroded preferences and losses of tariff revenues may be needed.

---

[53] Changes in national income are expressed in per cent of initial GDP, if not stated otherwise.
[54] Gains of 1.2 per cent or 365 bn dollars in the core scenario. For comparison, Francois et al. (1994) have estimated the Uruguay Round gains to some 291 bn dollars (in 1990 dollars), with a similar model but excluding services liberalisation.

Developing countries, including the LDCs, are the major winners of the simulated Doha scenarios. The results indicate that gains for developing countries, in proportion to GDP, are twice as large as for industrial countries (for LDCs three times). The developing countries' share in the total gains increases as more far-reaching liberalisation takes place. The largest share of these gains derives from trade facilitation.

Another conclusion is that a 'round for free' does not seem to be a valid concept. In other words, countries refraining from making commitments in the round may do so at a price. Trade liberalisation of developing countries benefits these countries the most, and the same applies to industrial countries. Moreover, the simulations underscore the importance of countries' own liberalisation. It is also concluded that countries with the highest trade barriers benefit the most from liberalising trade.

Global trade increases in all scenarios, from four per cent in the scenario with a lower level of liberalisation to 16 per cent in the one with more far-reaching liberalisation. The simulations also indicate that trade between developing countries rises particularly much, and that the developing countries' share of world trade increases with the level of liberalisation.

Of the four elements of the Doha simulations, trade facilitation is the one that contributes the most to global gains, followed by non-agricultural market access and agricultural liberalisation. According to the simulation results, liberalisation of services has the smallest effect. The size order of the negotiation areas' contribution to national income remains with more far-reaching liberalisation. However, with a lower level of liberalisation, market access for manufactures replaces trade facilitation as the key contributor to global gains.

The key role of trade facilitation that is indicated by the simulations is not surprising. First, this is the result of non-trivial commitments being modelled in this area, something which seems reasonable given the progress made in this area of the Doha negotiations. Second, costs of delays in trade caused by cumbersome border procedure are considerable. The results indicate that reform of cumbersome border procedures for trade in manufactures and agricultural goods leads to national income gains for all regions in the study and can play a key role for development. Still, in order for developing countries, and especially LDCs, to be able to implement agreements on trade facilitation, substantial capacity building is required. Since such reforms would also benefit industrial countries, there are also economic incentives for contributing to the implementation of these reforms.

Industrial countries benefit more from liberalisation of manufactures trade than developing countries do. This is due to the assumption, in this study, of economies of scale in manufactures and processed food sectors. Of the sectors with scale economies that expand, most are located in industrial countries.

On agricultural liberalisation, the simulation results further indicate that agricultural liberalisation in industrial countries has no considerable effect on the national income of developing countries, on an aggregate level. First, however, when looking at a more detailed level, the individual regions or countries show diverging results. Second, for developing countries as a group, the share of agriculture in trade in goods has dropped dramatically over the last three decades, reducing the expected impact of trade liberalisation. Nevertheless, considering the importance of the agricultural sector for many developing countries and for development and poverty alleviation, these results underline the need for more far-reaching agricultural commitments. This is necessary in order to realise the potential of agricultural liberalisation to contribute substantially to the gains of developing countries.

As to the relatively small gains from services liberalisation, it should first be noted that small real market openings for services trade are modelled. Important gains from services liberalisation could be expected if more far-reaching commitments are made. Second, the market access to different countries and sectors is simulated to converge towards best practice, rather than to markets without any trade barriers at all, a difference compared to some previous studies. Third, the small gains in this study are partly attributed to the fact that FDI is not explicitly modelled.

REFERENCES

Anderson, K. and W. Martin (2005), 'Agricultural Trade Reform and the Doha Development Agenda', *The World Economy*, **28**, 9, 1301–27.
Anderson, K., W. Martin and D. van der Mensbrugghe (2006), 'Doha Merchandise Trade Reform: What is at Stake for Developing Countries?', *World Bank Economic Review*, **20**, 2, 169–95.
EU (2005), 'Making Hong Kong a Success: Europe's Contribution', Brussels (28 October).
Fernandez de Córdoba, S., S. Laird and D. Vanzetti (2004), 'Blend it like Beckham – Trying to Read the Ball in the WTO Negotiations on Industrial Tariffs', Trade Analysis Branch (UNCTAD, Geneva).
Francois, J., B. McDonald and H. Nordström (1994), 'The Uruguay Round: A Global General Equilibrium Assessment', CEPR Discussion Paper No. 1067 (London).
Francois, J., H. van Meijl and F. van Tongeren (2005), 'Trade Liberalization in the Doha Development Round', *Economic Policy*, **20**, 42, 349–91.
G20 (2005), 'G-20 Proposal on Market Access' (12 October).
Gibson, P., J. Wainio, D. Whitley and M. Boman (2001), 'Profiles on Tariffs in Global Agricultural Markets', USDA, United States Department of Agriculture, Washington (USA) 2001/01, *Agricultural Economic Report* (796).
Harrison, W. J., J. M. Horridge and K. R. Pearson (2000), 'Decomposing Simulation Results with Respect to Exogenous Shocks', *Computational Economics*, **15**, 3, 227–49.
Hertel, T. (ed.) (1997), *Global Trade Analysis: Modeling and Applications* (Cambridge University Press, Cambridge).
Kalirajan, K. (2000), 'Restrictions on Trade in Distribution Services', Australian Productivity Commission Staff Research Paper (Ausinfo, Canberra, August).
Matthews, A. and K. Walsh (2005), 'The Economic Consequences of the Doha Round for Ireland', Research Report prepared for *Forfás* (Department of Economics and Institute for International Integration Studies, Trinity College Dublin).
McGuire, G. and M. Schuele (2000), 'Restrictiveness of International Trade in Banking Services', in C. Findlay and T. Warren (eds.), *Impediments to Trade in Services: Measurement and Policy Implications* (Routledge, London and New York).

McGuire, G., M. Schuele and T. Smith (2000), 'Restrictiveness of International Trade in Maritime Services', in C. Findlay and T. Warren (eds.), *Impediments to Trade in Services: Measurement and Policy Implications* (Routledge, London and New York).

Nguyen-Hong, D. (2000), 'Restrictions on Trade in Professional Services', Productivity Commission Staff Research Paper (Ausinfo, Canberra, August).

OECD (2003), 'Quantitative Assessment of the Benefits of Trade Facilitation', Document TD/TC/WP(2003)31/FINAL (Paris).

Piermartini, R. and R. Teh (2005), 'Demystifying Modelling Methods for Trade Policy', WTO Discussion Paper No. 10 (Geneva).

Swedish Board of Agriculture (2006), Calculations Received by the Swedish National Board of Trade.

Swedish National Board of Trade (2003), 'Trade Facilitation from a Developing Country Perspective', Report.

Swedish National Board of Trade (2006), 'Economic Implications of the Doha Round', Report.

Warren, T. (2000), 'The Identification of Impediments to Trade and Investment in Telecommunications Services', in C. Findlay and T. Warren (eds.), *Impediments to Trade in Services: Measurement and Policy Implications* (Routledge, London and New York).

World Bank (2005), *Enterprise Surveys: Trade Data* (at http://rru.worldbank.org/EnterpriseSurveys/) (World Bank, Washington, DC).

WTO (2002), 'WTO Members' Tariff Profiles', Document TN/MA/S/4/Rev.1 (Geneva).

WTO (2005), 'Doha Work Programme, Ministerial Declaration, 18 December 2005', Document WT/MIN(05)/DEC.

7

Rethinking Trade Preferences: How Africa Can Diversify its Exports

Paul Collier and Anthony J. Venables

1. INTRODUCTION

TRADE preferences for developing countries continue to be a major part of the world trading system. Under the Generalised System of Preferences (GSP) developing countries have access to most OECD markets, and historical ties have been recognised in schemes such as the EU's Lomé and Cotonou agreements. Recent years have seen several major extensions of preference schemes. The EU's Everything But Arms (EBA) scheme, initiated in 2001, gave duty-free access to least developed countries (LDCs) in (almost) all products. The US introduced the African Growth and Opportunities Act (AGOA) in 2000, improving market access for eligible Sub-Saharan African (SSA) countries. The US also operates the Caribbean Basin Initiative and the Andean Trade Promotion Act.[1]

These schemes have two main elements. One is the trade preference – the granting of market access at reduced tariff rates and with less restrictive quotas, possibly going all the way to duty- and quota-free market access. The other is the constraints on participation. These define eligible countries and products, and also impose rules of origin (ROOs). There has frequently been a tension between these elements, with the constraints severely reducing the effectiveness of preferences as an instrument of economic development. These constraints are likely to be particularly important for manufactured products, and redesign of preferences is needed if they are to facilitate developing country participation in a globalised world trading system.

This work was supported by the UK ESRC-funded Centre for Economic Performance at the London School of Economics. Thanks to Stefanie Sieber for research assistance.

[1] Both the EU and the US also have regional integration agreements extending preferences on a reciprocal basis, and the EU is moving towards replacing its Cotonou agreements with such Economic Partnership Agreements. Our focus is on unilateral rather than reciprocal preferences, although some of our policy messages will apply to both.

The benefits of trade preferences accrue through two mechanisms. The one usually emphasised is a transfer of rent to recipient (developing) countries. Instead of being received by the developed country importer as tariff revenue or quota rent, the preference margin is instead transferred to producers in exporting countries. The magnitude of the rent transfer has been calculated by various researchers. A recent study estimates an upper bound (preference margins times the value of trade) of around $11 bn p.a., of which around $500 mn goes to least developed countries.[2]

However, preferences can also generate benefits through a second mechanism: there may be a significant export supply response, creating employment in developing countries. This is the focus of the present paper. While the rent-transfer mechanism depends upon the existing quantity of exports, the supply response mechanism depends upon the potential of unrealised opportunities. For Africa, which is our geographic focus, this distinction between actual and potential exports approximates to that between agriculture and manufactures. Africa's rents from trade preferences depend upon market access for its existing agricultural exports, whereas preferences in manufactures might enable the region to break into markets that it has scarcely entered. Of course, rents for agricultural exports will also generate some quantity effect. However, the potential magnitude of the quantity effect is far greater in manufacturing exports. One reason for the greater potential is liberation from diminishing returns to scale. Production of manufactures for the domestic market encounters diminishing returns due to the constraint of small market size. Traditional agricultural and resource-based exports encounter diminishing returns because of limited endowments of suitable land and hence declining resource base per worker. By contrast, employment in manufacturing exports can be expanded without running into diminishing returns to scale due to markets or endowments. The other reason for the greater potential is that manufacturing exports are subject to scale thresholds which can generate multiple stable equilibria. The scale thresholds arise because of well-documented external economies that advantage those firms that are located within a cluster of similar firms. Potentially viable export locations may be uncompetitive relative to established clusters and so never develop unless induced. Hence, not only may trade preferences in manufactures generate a large supply response, they may switch a location to a new equilibrium and so have permanent effects even if only implemented temporarily.[3]

---

[2] Hoekman et al. (2006) drawing on Low et al. (2005). See also Olarreaga and Ozden (2005) for an application to preferences in the apparel sector.

[3] Computable general equilibrium studies of trade preferences include both rent and supply effects, but typically ignore the potential of scale thresholds. See, for example, Karingi et al. (2007) for a recent example.

The importance of manufacturing and other modern sector exports to the wider process of economic growth is now supported by a good deal of evidence. The Asian experience is well documented, and a number of recent studies point to the role of exports in growth accelerations (Hausmann et al., 2005). Jones and Olken (2006) identify growth accelerations, and show that these are associated with an average 13 percentage point increase in the share of trade in income (over a five-year period) as well as an acceleration of the rate of transfer of labour into manufacturing. Pattillo et al. (2005) point to the association between growth accelerations and trade growth in Sub-Saharan Africa.

How can trade preferences be designed to maximise their effectiveness in stimulating a manufacturing supply response? The argument developed in this paper is that manufacturing supply response is not a simple matter of moving up a supply curve, but depends on a wide range of complementary inputs, some of which can be imported and some of which have to be developed domestically, often involving increasing returns to scale. Trade preferences can have a catalytic role, but will only perform this role if they are designed to allow import of complementary inputs, and to operate in countries with the skills and infrastructure to be near the threshold of global manufacturing competitiveness.

Our argument is based on several analytical strands of work and on empirical evidence from recent preference schemes. The analytical strands argue that modern sector export growth is characterised by 'fragmentation' of production and by increasing returns to scale, typically external to the firm. These ideas are developed in Section 2. Section 3 presents empirical work based largely on the experience of AGOA which, with relatively liberal ROOs in apparel, has seen rapid growth in exports of some participating countries. Section 4 draws conclusions, arguing that appropriately designed trade preferences can make a much more significant contribution to development than is suggested by existing literature.

2. MODERN SECTOR TRADE AND GROWTH

Modern sector production is not simply a matter of transforming primary factors into final output. It requires primary factors and many other complementary inputs, ranging from specialist skills and knowledge to component parts. These are frequently supplied by many different countries, with design, engineering, marketing and component production occurring in different places – a process known as fragmentation of production. Furthermore, productivity levels in these different activities are not exogenously fixed. They are shaped by learning and by complementarities with other activities. These processes often give rise to increasing returns to scale, and imply that clusters are more productive than is dispersed activity. We briefly review existing literature on both these aspects of modern sector production.

a. Fragmentation

Fragmentation – otherwise known as unbundling or splitting the value chain – refers to the fact that the different stages involved in producing a particular final good are now often performed in many different countries. Particular 'tasks' may be outsourced (or offshored) and can be undertaken in different places. This occurs in response to productivity or factor price differences, and may take place within a single multinational firm or through production networks of supplier firms.[4] Although widely reported, solid evidence on the extent of fragmentation is quite hard to obtain. A good survey is contained in Grossman and Rossi-Hansberg (2006), whose discussion includes the fact that the share of imports in inputs to US goods manufacturing has doubled to 18 per cent over a 20-year period. To put this number in perspective, the US is by far the world's largest economy so that opportunities for competitive domestic sourcing of inputs are evidently radically superior to those in the typical African economy.

Fragmentation means that comparative advantage now resides in quite narrowly defined tasks. For some products tasks may be undertaken in parallel and then 'assembled' in a single place. For others a sequential production process still applies, under which each task adds value to a product that crosses borders at each stage. In this case the partially complete product is an essential input to the task to be performed at the next stage. The effect of tightly restrictive ROOs is to prohibit participation in production processes of this type. Countries are unable to use preferences to exploit a comparative advantage in a narrowly defined task, instead having to undertake a wide range of tasks domestically to meet ROO requirements.

b. Increasing Returns to Scale and Market Failure

Analyses of market failures in manufacturing development have a long history. They underpinned much of the theory of shadow pricing developed in the 1960s and 1970s. More recently they have re-entered mainstream literatures on trade theory and industrial organisation with the development of models of trade with increasing returns to scale and models of complementarity and coordination failure.

Increasing returns to scale may be internal to the firm as costs fall with longer production runs and learning by doing. They are often external, meaning that firms in a particular location gain from the presence of other firms in related activities. One set of mechanisms creating these external returns to scale is technological externalities arising as firms learn from other firms, observing and borrowing best-practice technique. These technological spillovers have been extensively

---

[4] See Arndt and Kierzkowski (2001) for discussion of this, and for more recent treatments see Grossman and Rossi-Hansburg (2006) and Markusen and Venables (2007).

researched in the industrial organisation and spatial economics literatures, and they are typically found to be important, particularly in high-tech industries, and to be spatially concentrated. Notice that the knowledge discovered need not be sophisticated technology – it might simply be discovery of the fact that it is possible to undertake a particular type of business profitably in a particular location. This has a demonstration effect which underlies theories of social learning and which Hausmann and Rodrik (2003) have termed 'economic development as self-discovery'.

In addition to technological externalities there are a number of pecuniary externalities associated with provision of complementary inputs. As a cluster of firms grows so specialist input suppliers develop, markets for intermediate goods become thicker, transport and infrastructure support improves, and workers have a greater incentive to acquire skills.[5] For example, consider a downstream industry that requires specialist inputs from upstream firms, or specialist skills from its workers. If there is a single firm in the downstream industry there will be no incentive for upstream suppliers or workers to invest in improving quality or acquiring skills, since they will be 'held up' by the monopsony power of the downstream firm. The complementarity is evident; it is only once the downstream industry is large enough that there is an incentive for its suppliers to upgrade and thereby raise the productivity of the combined operation.

There is a good deal of empirical work establishing the importance of thick market effects. Productivity is higher in areas of dense economic activity, and work on cities suggests that, over a wide range of city sizes, each doubling of size raises productivity by 3–8 per cent (see the survey by Rosenthal and Strange, 2005). The effects often operate over quite a small spatial range – within a city or travel-to-work area. The benefits may be shared among a number of sectors (as with improved transport or more regular shipping services) but are often quite sector or task specific, as in sectoral clusters in financial services, film production or electronics.

An important consequence of spatially concentrated increasing returns is that comparative advantage is, in part, *acquired* rather than fundamental. A particular location may have no inherent advantage in a sector or task, but as a cluster starts to develop so costs fall, creating the comparative advantage.

c. Implications – Lumpy Development

The facts of fragmentation and of increasing returns to scale imply that modern sector export growth is likely to be uneven or 'lumpy' in three senses; in product space, in geographical space and in time. Lumpiness in product space arises as

---

[5] See Duranton and Puga (2005) for a survey of the microeconomic mechanisms underlying clustering.

the acquired comparative advantages of learning and clustering may be narrowly concentrated in a few tasks, implying that countries may come to specialise in a very narrow range of activities. Lumpiness in geographical space means that activity may be concentrated in small spatial areas – cities will acquire particular specialisations. And lumpiness in time means that there are threshold effects; establishing a new activity in the face of existing competition may be quite difficult, but once it gets established costs start to fall and growth can become extremely rapid.[6]

All three of these aspects of 'lumpiness' are illustrated by recent experience. Hausmann and Rodrik (2003) draw attention to the very narrow specialisation of many countries; both Pakistan and Bangladesh have more than one-quarter of their total exports concentrated in just three (different) six-digit product lines.[7] Spatial concentration is apparent from the rapid growth of urban areas and of clusters of activity (e.g. Henderson, 2002). An extreme example of product and spatial concentration is the city of Qiaotou, producing 60 per cent of the world's buttons. As for rapid growth, Bangladesh shipped its first consignment of garments to the US in 1978, had exports of $600 mn by 1990 and more than $6 bn by 2005, employing 2.5 million people.

What are the implications of these facts for a region with abundant skilled labour and low levels of both hard and soft infrastructure, such as Sub-Saharan Africa? Successful participation in production networks and fragmented production processes requires a business environment that delivers security, contract enforcement and protection from predation. It also requires a level of infrastructure that can support continuous production and reliable delivery. However, the fact of spatial concentration means that it is not necessary that high quality infrastructure be provided everywhere – it can be provided in selected areas or in special economic zones. This is positive for Africa since it economises on these scarce inputs. Infrastructure (and institutions) can be targeted so that some areas work well, and this is more efficient than spreading infrastructure at a uniformly low level.

The fact that globalisation enables countries to specialise on a narrow product or task range is also positive for Africa. Instead of having to learn and acquire comparative advantage in all stages of a product's production, fragmentation makes it possible to progress incrementally, first learning narrow tasks – such as production of a particular type of garment using imported textiles and yarn. However, barriers to trade in intermediate goods are a critical obstacle to this. The barriers may arise because of domestic import restrictions, because of high trade costs due to geography and infrastructure, or because of rules of origin. They all have the effect of inhibiting participation in global production networks.

---

[6] For further development of these ideas see Burgess and Venables (2004) and Puga and Venables (1999).

[7] The six-digit classification is highly disaggregated – e.g. one of Bangladesh's three categories is 'hats and other headgear – knitted or from textile material not in strips'.

The temporal lumpiness of modern sector growth is also problematic. Coordination failures mean that getting started is hard, and it is only once a threshold has been passed that increasing returns start to reduce costs. This calls for some sort of catalytic action to overcome initial obstacles and get to the threshold level.

d. Trade and Industrial Policy

What implications follow for trade and industrial policy in general, and trade preferences in particular?

Past African discussion of industrialisation strategies has generally focused upon the trade policies of African governments. Changes in African trade policy would indeed be a necessary part of catalytic action, but not in the form most commonly envisaged. For an African-based firm to succeed in exporting a manufacturing 'task' it would need to be able to import without restriction all the complementary upstream tasks. Hence, the catalytic trade policy for African governments is to remove their current tariffs on manufactured inputs. For example, in West Africa, ECOWAS imposes a uniform 10 per cent tariff on all such inputs. While 10 per cent may appear modest, suppose that in the absence of trade impediments an Africa-based firm would choose to import inputs constituting half of the value of its output, so that the tariff raises its total costs by five per cent. Now consider what this implies for what the firm can afford to pay as labour costs. Even in labour-intensive manufacturing, labour costs typically only constitute around 16 per cent of total cost. Hence, to keep its total costs constant in the face of the tariff on inputs, the firm would need an offsetting reduction in its labour costs to 11 per cent. Thus, to compete with firms based in a location that was identical other than that it did not impose tariffs on inputs the firm would need to pay wages that were around one-third lower. Of course, Africa's problem arises precisely because its locations are *not* currently identical to those of Asia – they have higher costs due to the lack of clusters. Tariffs on inputs intensify the problem rather than resolve it.

Should an astute government adopt a tariff structure with zero tariffs on inputs but positive tariffs on final goods? There are several reasons why such a strategy would also fail. First, the country's niche in the long chain of manufacturing 'tasks' that eventually generate a final product is unlikely to be precisely the final 'task'. For any task prior the protection would be useless. And products which are 'final' to one industry are 'inputs' to another industry. As the above examples demonstrate, modern manufacturing niches are so specialised that the domestic market for them in the typical African country is too small to be a significant inducement to relocation. How important is the prospect of a price premium in the Senegalese market for buttons in determining whether firms selling on the global market should relocate their production from Qiaotou? Even in the unlikely event that such protection would be significant, the political difficulties for the Senegalese government of imposing high tariffs on buttons alongside free trade in all the myriad inputs that button producers want to use would surely be overwhelming.

An alternative style of industrial policy for an African government would be to subsidise the costs of production rather than protect the domestic market. But such policies have a poor track record. As a claim on government expenditure it would have to compete with manifestly pressing social needs. Further, the most conventional form of subsidy, tax incentives for investment, subsidises capital and this can be at the expense of employment. Untargeted production subsidies would be expensive because existing production for the domestic market would qualify, but targeting requires information that is typically not available to government, and a degree of discretion that risks eliding into corruption.[8] Perhaps the most effective way of targeting a subsidy towards exporting firms is to provide good quality infrastructure for geographically-defined export zones, but since Asian governments already do this, it may be merely a necessary but not a sufficient condition for inducing relocation.

Unlike these forms of industrial policy, trade preferences in OECD markets are not under the control of African governments; like aid, they are an instrument of development policies under the control of OECD governments. However, they have some major advantages over the policies that are available to African governments to provide the (temporary) advantage needed to get cluster formation. First, they are relatively immune from recipient country political economy problems, since they are set by foreign, not domestic government. Thus, there is no way in which their level can be escalated in support of failing firms. Second, since trade preferences support exports, they offer a performance-based incentive – firms benefit only if they export. Firms therefore face the discipline – on quality as well as on price – imposed by international competition. Rodrik (2004) argues that this discipline was an important positive factor underlying the success of export-oriented strategies, as compared to import substitution. Finally, they are fiscally costless to African governments and virtually costless to OECD governments and so compete with neither government spending on social needs nor aid.

Is there any evidence that trade preferences have had a positive effect on modern sector production? Before answering this question we need to be clear about what effects we expect. Preferences will be valuable if countries are able to participate in fragmentation and production networks. This is facilitated by liberal ROOs and by geographical proximity, as well as by standard determinants of comparative advantage. Even if these circumstances are met, their effects

---

[8] See Rodrik (2004) for discussion of these issues.

might be 'lumpy' – concentrated in a few sectors, regions or countries, and only setting in above some threshold.

In the next section we present analysis of the effects of AGOA and EBA on exports, but before doing this it is worth reviewing experience under other preferential trade schemes. The most successful such scheme has been the EU itself, where newly joining countries have generally experienced rapid growth of exports and of income as a whole. However, the EU extends far beyond trade preferences and so schemes that are purely concerned with trade and apply to developing countries are more pertinent.

NAFTA has had a strong effect on Mexican exports to the US, with exports growing five-fold in 12 years. This has led to increased employment in the border region, although the controversial issue is whether it has had significant repercussions for the rest of the Mexican economy (Hanson, 2004). The ASEAN Free Trade Area has been relatively successful in enabling low-income members (Cambodia and Laos) to participate in production networks with the middle- and high-income members (Indonesia, Philippines, Malaysia, Thailand and Singapore). It is notable that the ROOs are relatively straightforward and allow for cumulation across a wide range of member countries (see Cadot and de Melo, 2007).

Mauritius is the only African country to have decisively penetrated global markets in manufacturing, in the process transforming itself from an impoverished sugar island to Africa's highest-income economy. Famously, this performance defied the forecast of Nobel Laureate James Meade that the country was condemned to poverty. Subramanian and Roy (2003) investigate the reasons for the take-off. They find that export manufacturing success was the foremost proximate reason for economic success. In turn, the success in manufacturing was triggered by two coincident strategies. The Mauritian government granted duty-free inputs for manufactured exports and Subramanian and Roy find this to have been quantitatively important. However, they find that the OECD decision to grant Mauritius trade preferences in garments through the Multi-Fibre Agreement (MFA) was even more important. Crucially, the MFA gave Mauritius privileged access to OECD markets relative to established Asian producers. The MFA ended in 2004 but Mauritius is now well-established in OECD markets and has gradually shifted to more complex manufacturing 'tasks'. The temporary preference scheme was thus critical in permanently transforming the Mauritian economy.

3. EMPIRICS: AGOA – A NATURAL EXPERIMENT

The cleanest 'natural experiment' which enables study of the effects of trade preferences – and in particular of ROOs – is the African Growth and Opportunities Act (AGOA) which gives trade preferences to African countries in the US market.[9,10,11] This offers duty-free access for a wide range of products. Importantly, AGOA is not restricted to LDCs, and is currently available to 38 African countries, including Kenya, Nigeria and South Africa.[12] AGOA ROOs are strict (varying across products, but generally with inputs having to come from the US or other AGOA countries). However, they were relaxed for apparel under the 'special rule' clause. This allows eligible countries to use fabric imported from third countries in their apparel exports to the US so that the ROO is just a 'single transformation requirement' (i.e. that the transformation from fabric to garment is undertaken in the eligible country). This special rule is temporary and has been renewed under a series of waivers, most recently in December 2006 when the expiry date of end 2007 was pushed back to 2012. The special rule now applies to 25 African countries (including Kenya and Nigeria, but not South Africa).

Study of the effects of AGOA is particularly informative, as it can be compared with the EU's trade preferences under the Cotonou agreement and EBA. These are in many respects similar, but (a) have more restrictive ROOs for apparel, and (b) a somewhat different country coverage, only Least Developed Countries being eligible. The rationale for this restricted eligibility is that they are the countries that need it most. However, being the most lacking in skills and infrastructure, they are also the African countries least likely to be near the threshold of global manufacturing competitiveness.

a. Descriptive Evidence

We focus attention on the apparel sector, Sub-Saharan African exports of which are illustrated in Figure 1. The solid lines give exports of apparel from the region, excluding Mauritius. Exports to the US and the EU (defined throughout as the EU15, see the Appendix) were of similar values during the 1990s, but since then exports to the US have quadrupled from $400 mn to $1.6 bn, while exports to the EU, including those under EBA have stagnated. The dashed lines give exports from Mauritius. Exports from Mauritius to the US have stagnated throughout the period while EU imports soared in the first half of the 1990s for reasons discussed above, and have been constant since.

The growth of exports to the US has been concentrated in a few countries, as illustrated in Figure 2. The bottom line is exports from Kenya, now amounting to some $270 mn p.a., and the difference between this and the line above is Madagascar, with

---

[9] See http://www.agoa.gov/ for details.
[10] Several other studies look at the effects of AGOA, notably Matto et al. (2003), Brenton and Ikezuki (2005), Frazer and van Biesebroeck (2005), Olarreaga and Ozden (2005) and Brenton and Ozden (2006), discussed more fully below.
[11] For comprehensive analysis of the operation of ROOs see Cadot et al. (2006) and Cadot and de Melo (2007).
[12] For details of eligibility see http://www.agoa.gov/eligibility/country_eligibility.html.

FIGURE 1
Apparel Exports from SSA, $Mn

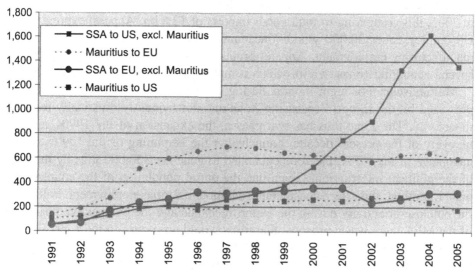

Source: UN Comtrade.

FIGURE 2
Apparel Exports to the US from SSA, $Mn

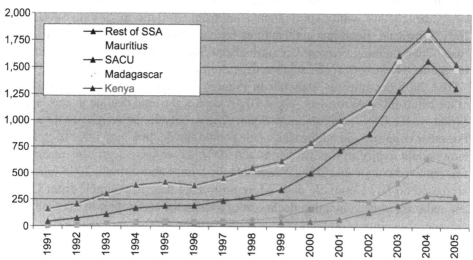

Source: UN Comtrade.

exports to the US of around $300 mn p.a. SACU exports have reached $700 mn p.a. and Mauritius's exports have held around the $250 mn p.a. level. The combined apparel exports to the US of all other SSA countries is only some $50 mn p.a., although within this there are some very fast-growing totals, such as Malawi.

b. Country Narratives

Kenya: Kenyan apparel exports to the US went from $40 mn in 1999 to $270 mn in 2005, this comparing to total goods exports of $2.8 bn. Apparel exports to the US employs over 30,000 workers accounting for 15 per cent of formal sector manufacturing employment. Apparel production is largely based in a number of special economic zones, within which it makes up 90 per cent of employment.

Madagascar: For eight months during 2002 political disturbance closed the port used by the Export Processing Zone and consequently drastically reduced its activity. The Zone thus has two phases, the expansion of the 1990s, and the recovery of the present decade. Launched at the beginning of the 1990s to take advantage of the MFA, the zone expanded to generate 300,000 jobs by the time of the political interruption. Given that the entire population of the country was only 15 million, this was a considerable addition to formal employment. Following the collapse of activity during the export blockade and the prospective phase-out of the MFA there was a prospect that firms would not return to the zone. Indeed, just as the MFA had produced a coordinated development of the cluster, the blockade produced a coordinated exit. However, AGOA was sufficient to trigger a strong recovery. Total exports of goods under AGOA are now $740 mn (of which apparel is $300 mn).

SACU: The position with SACU is given in Figure 3. Data for separate countries becomes available from 2000 (they are not all zero in 1999). Lesotho has been the largest beneficiary, with exports increasing from $140 mn in 2000 to $400 mn in 2005. Swaziland, Botswana and Namibia have all seen rapid growth from a smaller base. The remaining element is exports from South Africa which are not eligible for the ROO waiver. These stagnated before turning down sharply in 2005.

The 2005 downturn is apparent in Figures 1–3 and is largely due to the end of the Multi-Fibre Agreement. Some 70 per cent of the total decline in SSA apparel exports to the US is attributable to South Africa, outside the AGOA ROO waiver. For other countries, an additional factor behind the decline may have been uncertainty about expiry of this waiver at end 2007; as we have seen, this uncertainty was removed only at end 2006. Notice that the figures above run to 2005, since they are based on UN Comtrade data. More up-to-date data is available from USITC and indicates some continuing decline in exports in the earlier part of 2006 although the rate of decline is slowing.[13]

c. Econometrics

Although the raw data presented in the figures above is persuasive, we also present some econometric analysis. The simplest model expresses imports from

---

[13] http://www.agoa.info/index.php?view=trade_stats&story=apparel_trade.

FIGURE 3
Apparel Exports to the US from SACU, $Mn

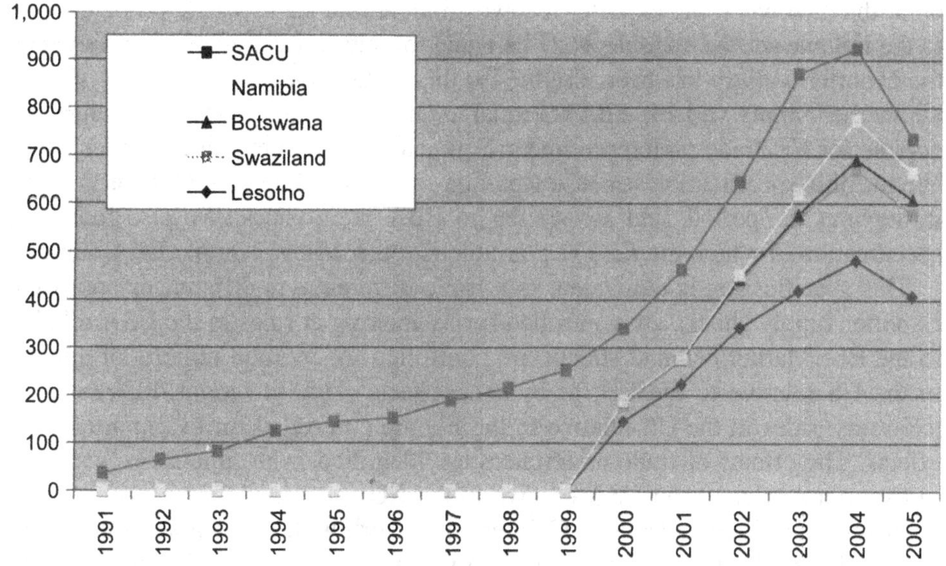

Source: UN Comtrade.

country i to market j, x_{ij}, as a function of some supplier country characteristics, S_i, some importer country characteristics, M_j, and some between-country charac-teristics, d_{ij}. All of these may be time-varying so writing the relationship for the two importer markets that we study, the USA and the EU,

$$x_{iUS}(t) = S_i(t)M_{US}(t)d_{iUS}(t)u_{iUS}(t)$$

$$x_{iEU}(t) = S_i(t)M_{EU}(t)d_{iEU}(t)u_{iEU}(t),$$

where $u_{ij}(t)$ is an error term. By focusing on performance in one export market relative to the other, supplier country characteristics can be substituted out, giving

$$x_{iUS}(t)/x_{iEU}(t) = [M_{US}(t)/M_{EU}(t)][d_{iUS}(t)/d_{iEU}(t)][u_{iUS}(t)/u_{iEU}(t)],$$

and this provides the relationship that we will estimate.

The dependent variable, $x_{iUS}(t)/x_{iEU}(t)$, is the value of apparel exports from country i to the US relative to this country's apparel exports to the EU. The relative market size element, $M_{US}(t)/M_{EU}(t)$, we capture by total imports of apparel to the US and the EU from all countries other than country i. We also run specifications where this variable is replaced by a year fixed effect. The relative between-country component, $d_{iUS}(t)/d_{iEU}(t)$, contains some fixed parts – such as distance and invarying trade preferences – and also the time-varying and country-pair specific trade preferences in which we are interested. We capture the constant parts by exporter fixed effects, and the time-varying parts by dummy variables which are switched on at the date when the exporter receives preferential trade benefits. For imports to the US, we set the variable *AGOAA* equal to unity for complete years in which the exporter country has been eligible for the AGOA apparel waiver. For the EU we set the dummy variable *EBANC* equal to unity for years in which a country not eligible for EU trade preference under Cotonou received preferences under EBA. We use this specification because Cotonou (and preceding Lomé) were in place throughout the period, and are similar to EBA preferences. We also look at a specification in which the *EBANC* variable is replaced by a simple EBA dummy.

This specification is equivalent to a triple difference-in-differences approach. Exporter supply shocks are controlled for by looking at sales in the USA relative to the EU. Market demand shocks are controlled for by total imports of apparel in the US relative to the EU, or by time effects. Time-invariant differences in exporters' sales in the US relative to the EU are controlled for by exporter fixed effects. The effects of trade preferences are identified from time-series variation in exporters' sales to the USA relative to the EU.

Results are given in Table 1. Columns 1–3 work with the sample of 86 developing and middle-income countries (see the Appendix), excluding those where apparel exports to the USA and EU combined averaged less than $1 mn p.a. over the period. We see that the AGOA apparel (*AGOAA*) provision has a positive and significant effect. A coefficient of 2 corresponds to an increase by a multiplicative factor of 7.4 (= exp(2)). In contrast, the EBA variables, both *EBANC* and simple *EBA* do not have a significant effect (and have the wrong sign).

TABLE 1
Apparel Exports to the US Relative to the EU, 1991–2005
Dependent variable: apparel exports to the US relative to exports to the EU, $\ln(x_{iUS}/x_{iEU})$

$\ln(x_{iUS}/x_{iEU})$	1	2	3	4	5	6
AGOAA	2.21	2.06	2.00	2.28	2.22	2.47
	(5.19)	(4.49)	(4.22)	(4.41)	(4.06)	(4.49)
EBANC	0.295	0.21		−0.58	−0.24	
	(0.52)	(0.36)		(−0.83)	(−0.33)	
EBA			0.14			−0.96
			(0.37)			(−2.52)
$\ln(M_{US}/M_{EU})$	1.14			2.15		
	(2.56)			(4.22)		
Year fixed effects	No	Yes	Yes	No	Yes	Yes
Exporter fixed effects	Yes	Yes	Yes	Yes	Yes	Yes
No. of observations	1,239	1,239	1,239	1,599	1,599	1,599
Countries	86	86	86	110	110	110

Notes:
Cols 1–3, exclude countries with mean apparel exports < $1 mn.
Cols 4–6, exclude countries with mean apparel exports < $100,000.

TABLE 2

Textile and Apparel Exports to the US Relative to the EU, 1991–2005

Dependent variable: apparel exports to the US relative to apparel exports to the EU, *relative* to, textile exports to the US relative to textile exports to the EU

$\ln(x_{iUS}/x_{iEU}) - \ln(y_{iUS}/y_{iEU})$	1	2
AGOAA	2.65	1.98
	(4.47)	(2.47)
AGOA		0.90
		(1.28)
EBANC		0.48
		(0.46)
Year fixed effects	Yes	Yes
Exporter fixed effects	Yes	Yes
No. of observations	1,024	1,024
Countries	71	71

Note:
Excludes countries with mean apparel or textile exports < $1 mn.

Columns 4–6 have a sample of 110 countries, adding in countries with mean apparel exports between $100,000 and $1 mn. Including these smaller countries causes a small increase in the AGOA coefficient. EBA effects now have the correct sign,[14] but it is only in the case where EBA is treated as an innovation with respect to Cotonou (column 6) that the effect is significant, indicating that it increases exports to the EU (relative to the US), by a factor of around 2.6 (= exp(0.97)).

Table 2 extends the analysis to a quadruple difference-in-differences. Suppose that the relative between-country component, $d_{iUS}(t)/d_{iEU}(t)$, varies over time because of factors other than trade preferences – for example, improving economic relations between the US and a particular country. If this effect is the same across commodity groups, then the AGOA apparel effect can be identified by looking at apparel trade relative to trade in some other commodity – we use textiles. AGOA affects both apparel and textile trade, but the AGOA apparel waiver operates for a smaller set of countries and (somewhat) shorter time period. In principle we can therefore separate out the effect of the AGOA apparel waiver from that of AGOA as a whole, while conditioning out shocks that affect both product classes.

Results are given in Table 2. The first column omits the simple AGOA and EBA (non-Cotonou) effects, since these should affect apparel and textiles in a similar way. The estimated AGOAA apparel effect is then highly significant, and of somewhat greater magnitude than we found in Table 1. Column 2 allows AGOA and EBA to affect apparel and textiles in different ways. We find that effects are insignificant, although the AGOAA apparel effect is brought back to a coefficient of 1.98, consistent

---

[14] A negative sign corresponds to an increase, since exports to the EU are in the denominator of the (logged) dependent variable.

with those in Table 1. This additional control therefore confirms the finding that the AGOA apparel treatment had a significant and large impact on apparel exports.

How do these results compare with others in the literature? Frazer and van Biesebroeck (2005) conduct an econometric study of US imports, working with a highly disaggregate commodity specification (at the six-digit level), but looking only at exports to the US market, and not therefore having the comparator of exports to the EU or any other market. They estimate a single equation across time, exporters and products, and use fixed effects to control for time-varying exporter and product effects, and (time-invariant) exporter-product effects. This involves 5.1 million observations and 850,000 fixed effects. The AGOA apparel effect is estimated to be highly significant, and accounts for a 51 per cent increase in trade. The likely reason that this number is so much smaller than our estimated effect is that we have the additional control provided by a comparison of exports to two markets. This enables us to have a time-varying fixed effect for each exporter which is specific to the commodity under study, apparel. This option is not possible for Biesebroeck and Frazer, lacking the control provided by a second import market.

4. CONCLUSIONS

For Africa to diversify its exports into manufacturing may require a catalyst to create clusters of activity and lift them to threshold productivity levels. Forty years of African domestic protectionism has failed to induce such clusters. However, the evidence suggests that – given the right conditions – it is possible for African countries to accelerate their modern sector export growth. Designing policy to promote such growth requires recognition of a number of features of modern global trade; fragmentation, increasing returns and the consequent lumpiness of development. Domestic policy and international policy are complements. Domestic policy needs to ensure a good business environment and infrastructure, but this can be spatially concentrated. International policy needs to redesign trading arrangements with rules of origin that do not penalise narrow specialisation. Two of the past initiatives in trade preferences for African manufactures, the MFA and AGOA, have both demonstrated their effectiveness. However, at the time when the MFA was launched few African governments had adopted the complementary policies needed for success, and the MFA has now ended. The key feature that made AGOA effective, the apparel special waiver, has now been renewed through to 2012, but AGOA applies only to the US market. The natural large market for Africa is the EU. At the minimum there is thus an opportunity for the EU to redesign its trade preferences to promote African economic development, aligning its trade instrument with its aid instrument. However, the goal should be an integrated scheme across the OECD that subsumes both EBA and AGOA and thereby minimises the information costs to exporting firms.

APPENDIX
Exporter Countries

Country	Table 1 Cols 1–3	Table 1 Cols 4–6	Table 2
Afghanistan	x	x	
Albania	x	x	x
Algeria	x	x	x
Argentina	x	x	x
Armenia	x	x	
Bangladesh	x	x	x
Benin		x	
Bhutan	x	x	
Bolivia	x	x	
Botswana	x	x	x
Brazil	x	x	x
Bulgaria	x	x	x
Burkina Faso		x	
Cambodia	x	x	x
Cameroon	x	x	x
Cape Verde	x	x	
Central African Republic		x	
Chad		x	
Chile	x	x	x
China	x	x	x
Colombia	x	x	x
Costa Rica	x	x	x
Croatia	x	x	x
Côte d'Ivoire	x	x	x
DR Congo		x	
Djibouti	x	x	
Dominican Republic	x	x	x
Ecuador	x	x	x
Egypt	x	x	x

Country	Table 1 Cols 1–3	Table 1 Cols 4–6	Table 2
Liberia	x	x	
Mongolia	x	x	x
Morocco	x	x	x
Mozambique	x	x	x
Namibia	x	x	x
Nepal	x	x	x
Nicaragua	x	x	x
Niger	x	x	x
Nigeria	x	x	x
Oman	x	x	x
Pakistan	x	x	x
Panama	x	x	x
Papua New Guinea		x	
Paraguay	x	x	x
Peru	x	x	x
Philippines	x	x	x
Moldova	x	x	x
Russian Fed.	x	x	x
Rwanda	x	x	
Samoa	x	x	
São Tomé and Principe		x	
Saudi Arabia	x	x	x
Senegal		x	
Seychelles	x	x	
Sierra Leone	x	x	x
Solomon Isles		x	
Somalia		x	
South Africa	x	x	x
Sri Lanka	x	x	x

APPENDIX *Continued*

	Table 1 Cols 1–3	Table 1 Cols 4–6	Table 2
El Salvador	x	x	x
Equatorial Guinea		x	
Eritrea		x	
Ethiopia	x	x	x
Gabon		x	
Gambia		x	
Ghana	x	x	x
Guatemala	x	x	x
Guinea		x	
Haiti	x	x	x
Honduras	x	x	x
India	x	x	x
Indonesia	x	x	x
Iran, Islamic Republic of	x	x	x
Jamaica	x	x	x
Jordan	x	x	x
Kazakhstan	x	x	x
Kenya	x	x	x
Kiribati		x	x
Kyrgystan	x	x	
Lao PDR	x	x	
Lebanon	x	x	x
Lesotho	x	x	

	Table 1 Cols 1–3	Table 1 Cols 4–6	Table 2
Sudan	x	x	
Swaziland	x	x	x
Syrian Arab Republic	x	x	x
Tanzania	x	x	x
TFYR Macedonia	x	x	x
Thailand	x	x	
Togo	x	x	x
Trinidad and Tobago	x	x	x
Tunisia	x	x	x
Turkey	x	x	x
Tuvalu	x	x	
Uganda	x	x	
United Arab Emirates	x	x	x
Uruguay	x	x	x
Vanuatu		x	
Venezuela	x	x	x
Yemen		x	
Zambia	x	x	x
Zimbabwe	x	x	x

Notes:
Importer countries:
USA.
EU15: Austria, Belgium-Luxembourg, Denmark, Finland, France, Fmr Dem. Rep. of Germany & Former Fed. Rep. of Germany/Germany, Greece, Ireland, Italy, Netherlands, Portugal, Spain, Sweden, United Kingdom.

REFERENCES

Arndt, S. and H. Kierzkowski (eds.) (2001), *Fragmentation; New Production and Trade Patterns in the World Economy* (Oxford: Oxford University Press).
Brenton, P. and T. Ikezuki (2005), 'The Value of Trade Preferences for Africa' (processed, World Bank).
Brenton, P. and C. Ozden (2006), 'Trade Preferences for Apparel and the Role of Rules of Origin – The Case of Africa' (processed, World Bank).
Burgess, R. and A. J. Venables (2004), 'Towards a Micro-economics of Growth', in F. Bourguignon and B. Pleskovic (eds.), *Accelerating Development: Annual World Bank Conference on Development Economics* (New York: World Bank and Oxford University Press).
Cadot, O. and J. de Melo (2007), 'Why OECD Countries Should Reform Rules of Origin', CEPR Discussion Paper No. 6172.
Cadot, O., A. Estevadeordal, A. Suwa-Eisenmann and T. Verdier (2006), *The Origin of Goods: Rules of Origin in Regional Trade Agreements* (Oxford: Oxford University Press).
Duranton, G. and D. Puga (2005), 'Micro-foundations of Urban Agglomeration Economies', in V. Henderson and J. Thisse (eds.), *Handbook of Urban and Regional Economics*, Vol. 4 (North Holland, Amsterdam).
Frazer, G. and J. van Biesebroeck (2005), 'Trade Growth following AGOA' (processed, University of Toronto).
Grossman, G. M. and E. Rossi-Hansberg (2006), 'The Rise of Offshoring: Its Not Cloth for Wine Any More' (processed, Princeton).
Hanson, G. (2004), 'What Has Happened to Wages in Mexico since NAFTA?', in T. Estevadeordal, D. Rodrik, A. Taylor and A. Velasco (eds.), *FTAA and Beyond: Prospects for Integration in the Americas* (Cambridge, MA: Harvard University Press).
Hausmann, R. and D. Rodrik (2003), 'Economic Development as Self-discovery', *Journal of Development Economics*, **72**, 2, 603–683.
Hausmann, R., L. Pritchett and D. Rodrik (2005), 'Growth Accelerations', *Journal of Economic Growth*, **10**, 4, 303–329.
Henderson, J. V. (2002), 'Urbanization in Developing Countries', *World Bank Research Observer*, **17**, 1, 89–11.
Hoekman, B., W. Martin and C. A. Primo Braga (2006), *Preference Erosion: The Terms of the Debate* (Washington, DC: World Bank).
Jones, B. and B. Olken (2006), 'The Anatomy of Start-Stop Growth', NBER Working Paper No. 11528 (http://www.econ.brown.edu/econ/events/startstop.pdf).
Karingi, S. N., R. Perez and H. B. Hammoudah (2007), 'Could Extended Preferences Reward Sub-Saharan Africa's Participation in the Doha Round Negotiations?', *The World Economy*, **30**, 3, 383–404.
Low, P., R. Piermartini and J. Richtering (2005), 'Multilateral Solutions to the Erosion of Non-reciprocal Preferences in NAMA' (WTO, Geneva).
Markusen, J. R. and A. J. Venables (2007), 'Interacting Factor Endowments and Trade Costs: A Multi-country Multi-good Approach to Trade Theory', *Journal of International Economics* (forthcoming).
Mattoo, A., R. Devesh and A. Subramanian (2003), 'The Africa Growth and Opportunity Act and its Rules of Origin: Generosity Undermined?', *The World Economy*, **26**, 6, 829–51.
Olarreaga, M. and C. Ozden (2005), 'AGOA and Apparel: Who Captures the Tariff Rent in the Presence of Preferential Market Access?', *The World Economy*, **28**, 1, 63–77.
Pattillo, C., S. Gupta and K. Carey (2005), 'Sustaining Growth Accelerations and Pro-poor Growth in Africa', IMF Working Paper No. 05/195.
Puga, D. and A. J. Venables (1999), 'Agglomeration and Economic Development: Import Substitution vs. Trade Liberalisation', *Economic Journal*, **109**, 455, 292–311.
Rodrik, D. (2004), 'Industrial Policy for the 21st Century' (processed, Harvard, http://ksghome.harvard.edu/~drodrik/UNIDOSep.pdf).

Rosenthal, S. S. and W. C. Strange (2005), 'Evidence on the Nature and Sources of Agglomeration Economies', in V. Henderson and J. Thisse (eds.), *Handbook of Urban and Regional Economics*, Vol. 4 (North Holland, Amsterdam).

Subramanian, A. and D. Roy (2003), 'Who Can Explain the Mauritian Miracle?', in D. Rodrik (ed.), *In Search of Prosperity* (Princeton, NJ: Princeton University Press).

Index